MANTLED
WITH A
KINGDOM PURPOSE

UNDERSTANDING YOUR IDENTITY IN CHRIST
FOR LIFE ON EARTH

J. NICOLE WILLIAMSON

Foreword by Jim Hodges

KING'S LANTERN PUBLISHING

ENDSORSEMENTS

I know of no better author and Bible teacher than J. Nicole Williamson. Her keen ability to see into the spiritual realm and discern the times and seasons of God makes her teaching gift one of the most accurate in the body of Christ today. The insights she shares in her latest masterpiece, *Mantled with a Kingdom Purpose*, will not only change your life, but will position you prophetically in the new thing God is doing. Don't miss your opportune moment! Get a copy of her book today.

Brandon Burden, Lead Pastor
KingdomLife Christian Center

Mantled with a Kingdom Purpose is perhaps the greatest master work written by J. Nicole Williamson. There has been no other time in global history whereby human identity and purpose have been under more intentional assault than now. We are being forced by evil to accept and affirm identities that are not only distorted and deceitful, but are demonically inspired. Thanks be to Father that the enemy of our souls is a defeated foe.

Nicole not only describes the manner in which these assaults are being perpetrated in culture, but she submits sound, relevant, and practical biblical principles that disarm and reverse these evil agendas through Kingdom understanding and action. This book is filled with insight, relevance, hope, and encouragement for all the sons and daughters of God to arise and become victors in this time. Once you begin to read this amazing book, you will not put it down until you have read it entirely. Well done my precious friend!

Apostle Larry Burden
KingdomLife Christian Center

In this treatise, *Mantled with a Kingdom Purpose*, Nicole Williamson exhaustively unpacks **who** we are so that we can effectively accomplish our **why**. Nicole takes us on a journey of our Kingdom origin that equips us with truth to discover our identity given by God before the foundation of the world. In the midst of the chaos and confusion centered around individual identity, this is absolutely a lighthouse in the fog and a "Now Word." My friend, Nicole Williamson, brings clarity to the imperative kingdom truth of who and why we are here.

Anthony Turner, President
Destiny Ministries International

We are living in unprecedented times and a pivotal moment in history for the Body of Christ. Now, more than ever, we need to be secure in who we are as sons and daughters of the Almighty God. *Mantled with a Kingdom Purpose* brings the truth that counters the lies and deceptions holding many believers in bondage today. As usual, Nicole's in-depth insight into the subject at-hand makes this book a must-read for everyone who wants to grow in their walk with Jesus. *Mantled with a Kingdom Purpose* will inspire you, challenge you, and most importantly transform you to live out who you are in Christ to accomplish His will for your life.

Rocky Byers
President, RBM
Pastor, Next Level Church

TABLE OF CONTENTS

To my children, grandchildren, and the generations that follow. May you be intimately acquainted with the Father, Son, and Holy Spirit, seeking His Kingdom first in everything. May you know who you are and why you are here, and may Abba's blessing rest on you in every way. May you seek to know His glory and glorify Him in all things. You are loved.

"But truly, as I live, all the earth shall be filled
With the glory of the Lord."
Numbers 14:21 (NKJV)

FOREWORD

This excellent book is a comprehensive manual for educating and activating the body of Christ to receive its mandate from the Lord God of heaven and earth in order to function in its divine purpose to extend the Kingdom of God into all the spheres of life on earth in the here and now!

Since the Kingdom of God is present and eternal, you and I are called and equipped to engage, declare, and disciple all the nations of the earth so that the promise to Abraham regarding his seed, that is Christ, would bless all the nations of the earth! (Galatians 3:16 & Matthew 28:18-20).

Nicole begins where we must all begin, namely, knowing our identity in Christ! Sometimes, we need to be reminded that this is how Jesus of Nazareth began His ministry. At His baptism, while the Holy Spirit was descending upon Him, the Father spoke from heaven and said, "This is My beloved Son." This is *identification*. Father also said, "I am very well pleased with Him." This is *affirmation*. When the Spirit arrived as a dove and lighted on Jesus, we then witness the *impartation* that launched Jesus' public ministry.

I know you will discover and greatly appreciate the author's outstanding teaching gift. You will also be impacted by her strong prophetic anointing which accompanies her teaching of the Word of God.

I, for one, am impressed by the theological depth of this book. We, the body of Christ, need to be reminded of the agenda of our Exalted King to see comprehensive transformation in human cultures, societies, and nations. Instead of seeking to escape the earth, or thinking the earth will be destroyed, we need a prophetic wake-up call that we are summoned and equipped to be planet managers. We do this by walking and ministering in the following callings: (1) as priests; (2) as prophets; and (3) as kings. This includes ladies, too! Adam and Eve both walked in these before their Fall. The Lord Jesus, the second Adam, walked in them. Now, we, His Ekklesia Church, are to walk in them!

I believe this book will advance the Body of Christ in all the God-inspired goals which have now come into focus for God's people in this hour. These include – revival, the Third Great Awakening, the global Kingdom Harvest, the rising of the Ekklesia (the Church) to be the vessel of God's Kingdom Government in the earth, and of the manifestation of God's glory of God in the 7 mountains of culture which shape the nations.

I encourage you to read, study, pray, and apply the truths from this revelatory book to enhance your personal growth. Use it as a manual on how to practically function in your Kingdom assignment. Employ this book in teaching and for inspiring followers of Jesus!

Jim Hodges
Founder and President
Federation of Ministers and Churches International

INTRODUCTION

I am convinced that one of the greatest needs of Christians today is to understand their identity and purpose in Christ. Satan's weapon of deception has not only cut off humanity from a true identity as God's created image, but has suppressed the truth of the believer's authority and commission as Christ's Body. That commission involves the anointing and mantle of identity, purpose, and gifts given us to accomplish the works of God in the earth (Eph. 2:10).

Satan fears our awakening to who we are in Christ, for when we do we will dismantle his evil agendas.

The spiritual blindness and passivity that has crept over much of the Church is the result of many things, including the abandonment of a biblical worldview, misguided doctrines that suppress the work and person of the Holy Spirit, and a hopeless eschatology.

According to recent research by George Barna, only 17% of American Christians now hold a biblical worldview, with only 37% of pastors themselves holding a biblical worldview.[1]

Barna research also found among practicing Christians that:

- 61% agree with ideas rooted in New Spirituality (collective consciousness and universal oneness).

- 54% resonate with postmodernist views (rationalism and morality based on individual views rather than Scripture).

- 36% accept ideas associated with Marxism (ideas that are anti-biblical).

- 29% believe ideas based on secularism (that meaning and purpose come from the material world).

- 28% strongly agree that "all people pray to the same god or spirit, no matter what name they use for that spiritual being."

- 27% believe that "meaning and purpose come from becoming one with all that is."

These statistics come from professing Christians. It shows how far the Church has drifted from the absolutes of divine truth, and from an identity of being a spiritual Bride whose thoughts are congruent with Christ's. Such deception within Church culture has cultivated passivity, compromise and a crossless life filled with distractions, sin, and bondage.

It has kept many from understanding and engaging the Father's purposes for their own lives, and their role in this world. It has kept many in a struggle of faith towards God and a true belief about themselves. It has limited salvation to a relationship with God, yet without the responsibility to carry that intimate fellowship into culture.

It has left the Church powerless and uninvolved in the world we are here to *cultivate* and *keep* through the love of God and the knowledge of His glory.

It has shaped the Church, Christ's Bride, as being in the world and of the world.

Nevertheless, I believe this is about to change. While Satan works on a global reset of evil proportions, the Lord Jesus Christ remains King of all with a glorious plan and reset of His own. The earth, after all, belongs to Him. His cross, resurrection, and ascension has already won the eternal triumph. He is now awakening His Bride, the Church (His *Ekklesia* – original Greek term for Church), to know her place with Him for the well-being of nations.

JESUS' HEAVENLY AND EARTHLY ARMY

While darkness rages all around us, that is not all that is happening. If all we are seeing is what the devil is doing in this cosmic battle then we must look again…for here comes the King, the Lord of armies, roaring from Zion! With Him is the heavenly host *and* His Bride – the Ekklesia – moving as one with Him for His purposes in the nations.

This Bridal company of the Last Adam is awakening to her true identity and purpose in Jesus. They have ripped off their blinders and are dressed for war. They have put on their spiritual armor and the Spirit of understanding regarding their position on earth. They are those being transformed from sheep into majestic war horses (Zech. 10:3).

They have embraced their mantle of true identity, calling, and anointing to do Kingdom exploits.

The glory of God prophesied to cover the earth will take place and each of us has a part in this royal decree. As the Bride takes her place, we are now seeing fresh voices emerge in the battle for the destiny of humanity. Many are mobilizing with renewed vision in true worship for revival, and reformation. We've had enough of the devil's schemes!

JESUS IS RAISING UP A MIGHTY GIDEON ARMY TO TAKE BACK THE LAND FROM THE DEVIL.

Jesus is sweeping out His House from ungodliness, as the Holy Spirit pours fresh fire on God's sons and daughters to run with renewed purpose to restore truth and justice in the streets. He is breathing into dry bones and breaking us free to move with courage for dismantling corrupt works in every sphere of culture.

He is raising a mighty Gideon army to take back the land from the devil.

THE CALL TO LABOR FOR THE HARVEST

Jesus said, *"The harvest is great but the laborers are few. Pray then that the Lord of harvest will send laborers into His harvest."* (Matt. 9:35-38)

We are about to enter the greatest harvest of souls in world history ... and a harvest requires workers. Jesus has planned for this harvest! He is now sending a fresh outpouring of His Spirit to reform how we, His Body, relate to His desires as the Lord of the harvest and to the harvest field around us.

We are being conformed to His likeness as ministers of revival and reformation.

He is opening our eyes to see this world as He sees it, and move with action for its destiny.

As Christ's Bride, we are being positioned in new assignments with new mantles and a fresh anointing. We are learning new mindsets – to have His mind in all things. He is sending us as kings and priests into the world to raise up ruined places and restore what has been destroyed. He is drawing hearts unto Himself in a great outpouring of His glory.

Jesus is saying, "I am involved, so get involved!"

SEEK FIRST THE FATHER'S KINGDOM

Jesus instructed His disciples to *"seek first the Kingdom of God and His righteousness"* (Matt. 6:33). The word *seek* here means: *to desire, go after, think about, and enquire about*. To seek for something requires a focused attention. To seek God's Kingdom is to seek the manifestation of His presence and His governance in all things. It is to seek for *Him* to be glorified in all things.

That seeking includes our worship, our words, and our actions to host His presence in every circumstance.

The Son's priority was, is, and will be to see the Father's glory and government manifest on earth. As His Bride, the Father's Kingdom is to be our priority, too. Our purpose is to *go after* the appearance (manifestation) of God's glory in every realm of life and society. His glory causes everything to flourish with righteousness, peace, and joy! Wherever evil is ravaging lives, that is where we must intercede and intervene for God's Kingdom of light to be displayed.

This passion to see God's glory manifest springs from the heart of the Son who loves the Father. Listen to His words:

"Our Beloved Father, dwelling in the heavenly realms, may the glory of Your name be the center on which our lives turn. Manifest Your Kingdom realm, and cause Your every purpose to be fulfilled on earth, just as it is in heaven." (Matt. 6:9-10, TPT)

God's glory, dominion, and purpose are intertwined. Earth was created to mirror heaven and we have been given charge of the earth (Gen. 1:26; Ps. 115:16).

As the Father's sons and daughters, the glory of His name is to be the centrality of who we are, and everything we do. It is central to our identity as His family. It is central to the mantle of purpose and anointing we carry – not as something to be relegated to a future event but as a "now" identity and authority.

God's glory is central to His every purpose being fulfilled in our lives and communities.

The nations are in a time of great spiritual warfare like no other time in history. The absence of light, love, and truth in culture has resulted in a fearful, hopeless, and violent society. We are in a time as *in the days of Noah*. Demonic strongholds have been erected in every sphere of culture and are reaping destruction in the lives and minds of men, women, and children. Fear, suicide, and a crisis of mental health are at an all-time high. Portals of demonic activity have been opened wide into human affairs.

As Jesus' Body we have been given the keys to close hell's portals into human affairs. It begins with rebuilding the altar of the Lord in our personal lives *and* at the gates of society.

For our nation to be healed, we each have a significant role assigned us in this matter. You and I have a part to play in the destiny of nations. For this we must put on the mind of Christ and enter the hour of greater works with Him. It is hell's lie that we are to be silent and kept out of societal influence!

It's time for the light within us to shine beyond us and break the strongholds of darkness in the world around us.

THE CALL OF GOD ON THIS GENERATION

The early apostles were known as *"those who turned the world upside down."* What will this generation of Christians be known for? Will history write about us as those who knew their God and did exploits? Will we be known as those who believed God and whose faith moved mountains? Or will we be known as those who hid their light and did nothing with what God gave us?

Darkness is increasing, and so must the light. At the time of this writing Texas is mourning the massacre of 19 children and 2 adults at an elementary school in the city of Uvalde at the hands of a lone gunman. What is a worse atrocity is that 19 police officers were told to *stand down* while the gunman continued his rampage. They did so ... willingly. Mothers who tried to intervene were handcuffed.

We are at the point in our nation that we must pray *and* take bold action for His glory to be revealed, souls saved, and culture transformed. We must shed passivity and silence. We must pick up the mantles of our identity given us in Christ and minister His presence and power to the world around us. We must run to the battle mantled with the anointing that sets captives free.

Pray with me: Father, thank You for all that You have given us as Your sons and daughters. Help us to step fully into the divine calling and mantle You have placed on us for such a time as this. May our lives count in the pages of history as those who dared to believe Your truth and act on it. Today may we be known as those who carry Your love and the glory of Your name as the center of our lives. In Jesus' name. Amen.

1

THE SIGNIFICANCE OF YOUR IDENTITY

*"We have become His poetry, a re-created people that will fulfill the
destiny He has given each of us, for we are joined to Jesus, the
Anointed One. Even before we were born, God planned in advance our
destiny and the good works we would do to fulfill it!"*
Ephesians 2:10 (TPT)

I t was a typical, sunny Texas day. Opening the door of my
home office, stood a well-dressed woman before me whom
I guessed to be in her late sixties. She had come for some
personal ministry. Taking a seat, she began to pour out her
story. Desperation laced her words. Her circumstances were
difficult, her challenges were many, yet her greatest expressed
pain in that moment was, "I don't know who I am."

Her words took me back to a moment, years prior, when I sat
in a pastor's office overwhelmed by an event that had taken
place. It was a repeated pattern in my life regarding an inward

response to people's negative words and actions towards me. I knew I was loved and accepted by God, but my value was a different issue. Assessing my state-of-being, my pastor looked at me and said, "Nicole, you don't know who you are!" His words stunned me. *How could that be? I had walked with the Lord for many years. I had experienced divine deliverance in my life. I was in ministry as a worship leader. I knew God's Word and presence.* But there I was, similar to the woman who now sat before me.

I followed the pastor's suggestion that day and went to a Christian counselor who ministered in inner healing. It was there I experienced a life transforming encounter with Abba Father, with *Papa.* It was an encounter that rooted me, like never before, in an identity as my Father's daughter. I didn't realize it then, but I'd just been given an important key that would impact my destiny. It's a Kingdom key that Jesus has given all believers through His death and resurrection.

WHO ARE YOU?

The two most asked questions by all humanity are: *who am I and why am I here?* The plants and animals don't seek to know these things. They are human questions.

That pain of longing to know personal identity and value is one I've heard through countless others of all ages, all social status, and all races. It is a question relentless in its quest to find the answer, feeling that somehow it will give meaning to everything else in life. We were created with great meaning, and we want to know what it is.

The answer to our identity and purpose is like an anchor to the soul in the midst of a storm. It is the light that leads us through dark places in life. It comforts us when we feel alone. That answer is the Father's love and presence that lets us know we are here because He planned for us to be here, we come from Him, and

He is near even when we can't see Him. The answer to our identity is found in Father's voice reassuring us that we are going somewhere – somewhere significant, because we are significant. Because we are His child.

We are significant to God *and* to His purposes with the world around us ... even when it may not feel that way.

Our identity and purpose are significant and have value because we were created in God's own image. The pain we feel when those questions of *who* and *why* go unanswered springs from the destiny implanted in us by our Creator longing to emerge and flourish with life. It is eternity itself beating in our hearts (Ecc. 3:11).

As my ministry partner and I prayed for the woman who came seeking help that day, we watched with joy as the Lord broke yokes of shame and rejection that had bound her soul. We watched as Jesus led her out of a dark prison of fear and into the light of His love, and true identity about herself.

> YOU ARE SIGNIFICANT TO GOD *AND* TO HIS PURPOSES WITH THE WORLD AROUND YOU.

God wants each of us to know how much He loves us, who we are *to* Him and *in* Him. He wants us to know our purpose with Him in this world. The Father has a will for our lives. He has a will for your life.

That *will* carries immense value – one that Satan hates and works to hide, suppress, or twist in every way he can. He is an expert in lies, deception, and manipulation. But God is greater and is ever working to bring us into all He has for us as His radiant sons and daughters.

To know *who* we are unveils *why* we exist. If the understanding of our *identity* is hidden or twisted, then understanding our *purpose* is also hidden or twisted. God wants us to know the truth about these matters – from race to gender to all of who we are as humanity in His image.

God defines who we are.

Not people, or their opinions.

Not money, things, or achievements.

Not philosophies of man or doctrines of demons.

Not Humanism, Darwinism, or twisted genderisms.

The Heavenly Potter, the Author, the Father is who defines our identity, worth, value, and purpose. Since these come from Him, they can only be defined by Him.

Being from Him, they are sacred.

HUMAN IDENTITY IS A SACRED THING

Jesus said, *"I know where I came from and where I am going"* (Jn. 8:14). He had no question about His identity and purpose. He came from the Father as the Word who returned to the Father having accomplishing what He was sent to do.

Knowing where we came from is key to where we are going in life. We came from God. We were in Him before the foundation of the world ... before we were in our mother's womb (Eph. 1:1-5). As those born of the Spirit, we carry the breath of God and we will return to the Father. Meanwhile, we are here to accomplish what we were sent here to do.

What did Father send you to do?

God brought you and I into the earth at an **appointed time** for an **ordained mission** to this generation.

We are here for a reason. A divine reason.

Our lives are significant and our missions are sacred because they come from God.

I want you to understand this because the devil works to dumb down everything about you and me as insignificant, random, illegitimate, disqualified, or less than. But here is the truth, you are significant and divinely deliberate. In Christ you are restored as a legitimate son or daughter, qualified by His blood, and are a priceless treasure in an earthen vessel.

God's Word says that Jesus was crucified *before the foundations of the world*, even before man's fall in sin. Father knew what would happen and had already prepared for our *full* restoration. No matter what we've been through, God's plans for us have never changed. He is working in you and me now to fulfill *all* that He has planned for us. For this world.

So, who are you, really? Let's look!

1 – YOU WERE CREATED AS GOD'S IMAGE ON EARTH

Genesis 1:26-28 says, *"And God said, **let Us make mankind in Our image, according to our likeness** and let them rule over the fish of the sea, and over the birds of the sky, and over the livestock and over all the earth, and over every crawling thing that crawls on the earth. So God created man in His own image, in the image of God He created him; **male and female** He created them. God blessed them; and God said to them, 'Be fruitful and multiply, and fill the earth, and subdue it; and rule over the fish of the sea and over the birds of the sky and over every living thing that moves on the earth.'"*

When speaking of something's *identity*, we are referring to the *set of qualities or characteristics* that define it. Since God made mankind in His image and likeness, mankind was created with a set of qualities and characteristics like God's. **Our Creator is the pattern of our original design**. We are not Him, but are patterned

23

after His likeness. Though sin marred our reflection of His image, we are restored in Jesus who is the *express image* of the Father (Heb. 1:3). To be in Christ, and Christ in us, is to be conformed to the original pattern of being the likeness of God on earth.

The word *image* (Heb. *selem*) means: *resemblance, representative figure, cut out of the same pattern, shadow, an exact replica, a **mirrored likeness***. Think about your own reflection when you look in the mirror. It looks just like you. You were created to mirror God in the earth. You are cut from the pattern of Himself and that is significant!

You and I are God's *image-bearers*. We are His *"shadow."* A shadow is something that moves with you when you move. Think about how your own shadow moves in unison with you. When you reach for a glass, it reaches for a glass. When you move to another room, it moves with you to another room. When you stop, it stops. It behaves how you behave. In other words, as God's "shadows" we move in unison with Him as He moves.

> YOU AND I ARE GOD'S IMAGE-BEARERS. WE ARE HIS "SHADOWS" WHO MOVE WITH HIM.

This is the concept conveyed, yet it is also much more.

This image-bearing shadow includes both movement and the inner qualities of the heart and its motives. That means we not only move *when* God moves, but we move *how* He moves, and *why* He moves. We move carrying His same heart, motives and intentions. We move because of His same Spirit in us. It is not a movement as puppets on a string, but as an agreement with Him in the bond of love.

When Jesus said to His disciples, *"Follow Me,"* (Grk. *deute opiso*), the idea conveyed was of *coming behind* so closely to Him that the one following was "covered in the dust" of His movement. This was the Jewish concept of being a disciple to a

Rabbi, learning a master's every move and way of thinking so that the likeness of the master was imprinted on the life of the disciple in every way. The disciple *shadowed* his master's heart and movement.

This is what Jesus is doing in conforming us to His own likeness as God's *image-bearers*. The word **likeness** (Heb. *d'mut*) means: *model, similitude, manner*. As God's likeness we are designed to model His manner and way of being. We move in union and unison with Him in heart, purpose, motive, and timing.

This beautiful relationship is designed to be expressed through the loving bond of a father and child ... as image and image-bearer. Jesus demonstrated this on earth. It's what He meant when He said, *"Truly, truly, I say to you, the Son can do nothing of Himself, unless it is something He sees the Father doing; for whatever the Father does, these things the Son also does in the same way"* (John 5:19). Moving with the Father was the natural flow of life for Jesus.

Jesus also said, *"For I did not speak on My own, but the Father Himself who sent Me has given Me a commandment as to what to say and what to speak"* (John 12:49).

When I first learned this, it explained a longing in my heart I'd had since I was a child – I wanted to walk with God. I would often tell Him so. I still do. It has been a compelling desire to know Him and be with Him in whatever He is doing on earth. To move with Him. I wanted His presence in my life, and to be close to Him. This longing is the eternal echo of original design as His image and likeness. It is our creation identity to be one with Him and move with Him.

Every human being has a place deep inside them that longs for closeness with the Creator. As we minister God's love to the people around us, we are shining the light into that eternal quest deep within them.

Our Father put eternity into us because we are eternal beings created to walk with Him, be close to Him, and be a part of what He is doing on earth ... to be His "shadows."

This should be our norm! In reality, it is *not* normal for anyone to move about and their *shadow* is still sitting!

2 – CREATED TO BE LIGHT IN THIS WORLD

God is light and Jesus is light. As Christ is in us then we, too, are light in this world (Matt. 5:14). We were created in His image as *light-bearers.* That light is His *glory. We* are *glory-carriers*. It is our original design restored in Jesus.

God's glory is the radiant essence of His being. His glory refers to the brilliance of His character, moral beauty and perfection, and power. It is the weightiness of His majestic splendor as being above all else.[1] When God breathed into man at creation, He breathed into him His radiant essence. He didn't do that with the animals. Just mankind. In doing this, God made us His "kind" so that we could have intimate fellowship with Him.

This is the breath of life and light returned to us in Christ.

God's glory is also the radiant fire of His love, for God is love and a consuming fire. As His image, we are carriers of His fiery love.

In my youth, I stumbled in deep darkness that nearly took my life. God sent me to a be under a ministry in Argentina that was experiencing God's glory and revival. I noticed they talked a lot about the light of God. I had been raised in Church, was saved, baptized in the Spirit, and had gone to Bible School, yet I was still in bondage and darkness. The realms of light they had was something I knew I didn't have, but I wanted it. It was the light of His manifest presence and glory.

Jesus answered my cry, and in that season He immersed me in the depths of His love and truth. It was *that* light that set me free.

The light of God's love and glory bring transformation because they bring us into truth, for God is truth and His truth is light. Love and truth draw the heart towards God. These are the qualities of God's glory that dwells in us who are in Christ.

Light is the great liberator from darkness and power to set people free. As *children of light*, we are *liberators* and *freedom agents*.

Today's world needs the light of God's love, truth and glory. Light brings hope. It brings new perspectives and possibilities. It brings heavenly solutions and joy. Light breaks the hold of darkness.

> LOVE AND TRUTH DRAW THE HEART TOWARDS GOD.

Today, American society is in darkness because of the lack of light and truth. Those in government need light. Education instructors and administrators need light. Those sitting in corporate boardrooms need light!

God is calling us – His light-bearers and glory-carriers – to move with Him to free lives and culture from the prison house of darkness.

3 – YOUR GENDER IS GOD-GIVEN

When God made mankind *in His image*, He made them male and female. Just two genders. It was an intentional plan, not random. It was simple, not complicated.

God is neither male nor female but in Him are both paternal and maternal qualities. He selected these qualities and gave them to us as part of our identity that represents His nature. God is a Father. He is also called El Shaddai – the "many breasted One" who is *more than enough to do what we cannot do*. God is strong yet gentle; He both disciplines and comforts. He is a Man of War (Ex. 15:3), yet hovers over His people like a mothering hen (Matt. 23:37). He is the beginning of life and the bearer of life.

Both male and female genders have beautiful and unique qualities. Gender is a gift from God. It is part of our representing Him in this world. This makes gender something sacred, honorable and significant. We love Him by loving who He created us to be.

Gender is hardwired into our physical, mental, and emotional DNA no matter what changes a person tries to make to their physical appearance.[2] The current assault on gender identity is Satan's work to destroy God's image on earth and confuse the innocent minds of children.

In 2019, statistics showed the rate of suicide attempts among adult transgenders was 40%, a percentage much higher than national averages.[3] Other sources say that transgenders are five times more likely to have attempted suicide than non-transgenders. "It's worse for transgender and 'nonbinary' youth with statistics that reflect 52% contemplating or having attempted suicide. Some blame this on rejection by others of their change, others on the failure to find peace from an internal conflict in the change they sought."[4]

GOD WANTS US TO EXPERIENCE THE JOY OF HIS GLORY IN OUR GOD-GIVEN GENDER!

The reality is that when we reject our authentic gender, we are rejecting ourselves.

Empowering self-rejection through body-altering drugs and surgery is to attack who we are. It affirms a lie believed about ourselves, and lies always bring us into bondage and darkness where there is torment.

Self-rejection destabilizes an internal sense of well-being. It creates an inharmonious frequency in the soul that wars against itself. Satan is the father of lies. We must pray and love those who are trapped in this lie – we must love them into the radiant truth of true identity.

To be deceived about such a fundamental part of personal identity is heart rending. The very essence of any lie or deception we embrace destabilizes the very foundation of a sound mind. The answer isn't to change body parts, but to exchange the tormenting lie for the love and truth that even our gender is an intentional part of our God-given identity. God wants us to experience the joy of His glory in our God-given gender!

The answer to this cultural chaos is God's love and truth, not silence or compliance. I have heard many testimonies of those who have escaped the trap of believing the lie that they were the wrong gender. The lie was often rooted in either a deep emotional wound, a search for acceptance, a stronghold of self-rejection, or social pressure. But the larger reason behind all of these is spiritual warfare against their lives. If this is you, know that God loves you and wants you to know the beautiful truth about yourself.

Psalm 139 says that God knit you (put you together) when you were in your mother's womb. He selected everything that makes up you – from physical to intellectual to spiritual traits. He put a calling on your life from before you even appeared on this earth. This means there is even a divine purpose in your authentic design of being male or female for fulfilling all that God has planned for you. Satan is a destiny-stealer, life-

> GOD ALONE HOLDS THE TRUTH OF WHO WE ARE AS MALE AND FEMALE.

killer, and peace-destroyer. His greatest weapon are lies that we perceive as truth, but are not. When lies become our "truth" it corrodes our soul, and everything else in our lives.

Sometimes I didn't like being a girl when I was growing up because of the way girls were portrayed on T.V. The social ideology at the time was that females should be timid, helpless, and do whatever they were told. To sit down and be quiet.

I grew up with 2 brothers close in age to me. My favorite game wasn't dolls but playing superhero. You can't be a superhero and be timid, helpless, or do whatever you are told. You certainly can't save the world sitting down and being silent! It wasn't a surprise when the feminist movement took hold, but they didn't have the godly answers that women needed either.

Religious culture itself has too often put women in an unbiblical box of silent servitude. No one likes silent servitude. That is not God's image. Females, too, were created to rule as God's likeness (Gen. 1:28).

God alone holds the truth of who we are as male and female. Males, too, often get wrong cultural and religious messages about who they are. We need girls to be girls and boys to be boys *God's way*, and to celebrate both. Over the years, I've had to break out of a lot of cultural and religious philosophy about who I am in order to step fully into the truth of who God made me as His image! Today I'm glad to be a Spirit-filled woman able to be bold, strong *and* gentle as I humbly submit to God's ways and carry His authority.

4 – YOUR ETHNICITY IS GOD-GIVEN

God holds the truth regarding everything about us, including ethnicity. Satan wants to steal the beauty of anything we carry as God's breath in earthen vessels. He made man from the ground

– dirt that He had created as the womb from which many life forms sprung to manifest the knowledge of Himself. The earth has many colors – from sandy soil, to beautiful brown and red soil, to rich black soil.

Humanity is one race, different colors and cultures, all designed by God. God loves them all, and all carry the same original design of being His image-bearers.

Our current *race war* in America is demonically inspired to tear us apart. We need to repent if we are sowing anything other than love and honor towards other people, no matter their color or gender. We must encourage one another's divine destiny. We must stop listening to hell's voice that promotes racial division. We must forgive wrong's done and move forward in grace together for the healing of our nation.

I recently heard a minister say that when he was growing up, he felt he could never fulfill his God-given destiny because of the color of his skin. Then he learned the truth! Today he travels the world fulfilling his destiny as an anointed worshiper, teacher, and apostle. I thought, *wow, and I grew up thinking I could never fulfill my destiny because of my gender!*

See, if it isn't one thing it will be another that Satan uses to lie to us and suppress us – some reason that we aren't good enough, or can't. We are the wrong color, wrong gender, wrong social status, or just wrong everything. Again, it's called *spiritual warfare*. Recognize it for what it is! The devil will find something to stop the celebration of who we are, or who others are ... until we learn the truth! We were created in God's image.

The Apostle Paul said, *"And have put on the new man, which is renewed in knowledge after the image of Him that created him: where there is neither Greek nor Jew, circumcision nor uncircumcision, Barbarian, Scythian, bond nor free: but Christ is all, and in all."* – Col. 3:10-11 (KJV)

5 – CREATED AS GOD'S "SEED"

Children are seed. As God's image-bearer in a clay vessel, you are His child, His seed in the earth. He created you to be His ruling lineage on earth as His son or daughter. You are the creation of His loving hands. In Christ, you are His righteous "seed" in the earth. Again, though sonship was lost by the fall it is restored in Christ through the Spirit of Adoption whereby we call God our *Abba Father* (*Papa*, Rom. 8:15).

I showed you earlier that the Hebrew word for *image* is *"selem." Selem* begins with the letter *tsade*, which speaks of *desire* and of *harvest*. **The very creation of humanity had within it the divine intention of a harvest.**

Father cares about the full harvest of what He created. He is passionate about the generations. Seed carries the identity of what *now is* and the potential of what *will be* at full maturity.

YOU ARE PART OF THE FATHER'S STORY!

Male and female Adam were the covenant seed, the beginning, of God's plan to *fill the earth with image-bearers. Their rule would be to cultivate earth so that it mirrored heaven.* God blessed them and commissioned them to increase in every way. They were seed that contained the seed of countless generations of *divine image-bearers governing the earth* and making it flourish with His glory! They were to reproduce God's *authority-bearers* in the earth.

You are part of that plan. You are part of the Father's story!

All seed carries the identifying characteristics of its origin. Just as a child carries certain characteristics of their parents, you carry qualities and unique aspects of God within you.

Those qualities include a myriad of things like personality, temperament, talents, and wisdom. It includes the ability to solve problems, imagine, create, communicate in diverse ways, release creative power through words, and much more. This is why you can never say that you are inferior or have no value. God's image in you makes you significant.

As a believer, you have a DNA that *Holy Spirit wants to empower fully* as the Father's *image-bearer* to minister His Kingdom on earth.

Your unique qualities and characteristics are both natural and spiritual. When God created mankind from earth's clay, even that clay held unique qualities that revealed the knowledge of the Creator. Romans 1:20 says that *God's attributes, eternal power, and divine nature, are clearly seen and understood by what He created.*

God took what "clearly" revealed Him and gave it something more – His own breath.

Mankind was created as a spirit being with a soul and put into an earthen body. This is what Father decided would be as His image, shadow, and representative.

Why is this important to understand?

YOUR IDENTITY AND PURPOSE ARE INHERENTLY LINKED TO THE EARTH AND TO GOD'S GLORY.

It means that your identity and purpose as a human being in God's image are inherently linked to the earth *and* to God's glory and power. Selah (think about that!)

You have a Kingdom identity and purpose linked to heaven and earth. So stop looking for the rapture to take you out of here! You have a divine work to do on earth.

Your calling is linked to the destiny of the land and to life on it.

As a born-again believer in Christ, you have been born of earth *and* born of the Holy Spirit. As you are about to see, your unique creation fits you for the will of God for your life. You are connected to both earth and heaven.

Satan has tried to pervert our understanding of these divine truths through many false ideologies such as Darwinism, Humanism, and LGBTQ⁺ agendas. It also includes the idea that we are just passing through our time on earth and our only focus is to make it to heaven. While we are *born from above* and our *citizenship is in heaven*, Scripture also says that we are *God's ambassadors* sent to reconcile earth with heaven.[5] We are created and gifted by God to do that. We are to use our time wisely here in doing the will of our Father.

You and I have a work to do as God's *image-bearers*. It is more than simply "being a good Christian." We are here to rule and govern the earth as His sons and daughters, not just when Christ returns, but here and now. It's imperative that we rise to our calling lest the harvest of souls and destinies of nations perish.

6 – CREATED AS A RULER

A ruler is someone who has authority for making decisions, giving verdicts, and making judgments within a specific jurisdiction. Ruling is another part of your God-given identity. You may or may not feel like a ruler, but that is part of being an image-bearer of the Most High. You carry a high calling, one restored in Christ. You are part of the body of the Ruler of nations. **It's time to think like who you are!**

Everyone has different capacities and spheres of ruling, but we are all created to govern. Ruling is an important part of our identity and purpose.

From the beginning, God created humanity to rule over His works. Psalm 115:16 says, *"The heavens are the heavens of the Lord, but the earth He has given to the sons of mankind."*

Psalm 8:4-6 says, *"What is man that You think of him, and a son of man that You are concerned about him? Yet You have made him a little lower than God, and You crown him with glory and majesty! You have him rule over the works of Your hands; You have put everything under his feet."*

Some versions of the Bible interpret this Scripture as man being made lower than angels, but the Hebrew word in Psalm 8 is not *angels* (*malak*) but *God* (*Elohim*). We are subject to Him, not to angels. Angels assist us in doing the will of God on earth.

Mankind carries not only a unique identity, but a role that is exclusive from the rest of creation. *Ruling is the delegated right with power to nurture, defend, and govern life so that it thrives to full capacity in the way God intends.* This is God's design for all who rule in any capacity.

A ruler oversees the destiny of a seed and takes action regarding God's intentions with it. This was established in Eden. Since God is love, ruling is an act of love, not tyranny.

I hope I have laid a simple yet clear foundation for you regarding identity – one that is both personal in your relationship with God *and* that links you to the world around you. In the chapters ahead, I will continue to unveil more of your purpose and calling as the Father's son or daughter in the various spheres of culture.

The Apostle John said, *"As He is, so are we in this world."* (1 Jn. 4:17)

Pray with me: Father, teach me to celebrate who I am in You as Your cherished child. Root me deep in Your love so that I am unwavering in my true identity in You. Teach me to shadow Your movement as You work to fulfill Your purposes in me, my family, my region, and nation. In Jesus' name. Amen.

To Ponder:

- *How significant do you feel your life is?*
- *How thankful are you for your God-given gender and ethnicity?*
- *How are you embracing your leadership role in caring for the earth?*

2

Living Your Kingdom Purpose

*"And the LORD God took the man, and put him into the garden of Eden to **cultivate** it and to **keep** it." –* Genesis 2:15

While identity involves the *defined qualities* of who you are, purpose is the *defined mission* for which those qualities are given. Only when you know your true identity can you know your purpose, since purpose springs from identity. Purpose carries a vision of how your God-given calling is to function in this world.

Do you have a vision from God for your life? What is it? If not, ask Him. God is a visionary who has created you for a purpose. Purpose is what God desires to accomplish through you in your ruling assignment on earth.

Purpose puts your identity in motion for doing Kingdom exploits!

However, there is one more thing you have been given in Christ for you to function *fully* in your Kingdom purpose – that is the anointing of the Holy Spirit. That anointing is the supernatural part of your abilities. It is like a mantle on your inner man. It is the abiding of God's Spirit in you to do above and beyond what you are able to do. It is the power of God in you and through you as God's son or daughter.

PURPOSE PUTS YOUR IDENTITY IN MOTION FOR DOING KINGDOM EXPLOITS!

Rulers, such as kings, wear robes or mantles that signifies the authority and role they carry. Revelation 1:6 says that you are a king and a priest unto the Lord. That is your purpose on earth. You are anointed for your purpose. Where did that purpose come from? Genesis 1:26 and 2:15 – *the command to rule, cultivate and keep.*

When creation beheld the man and woman in the Garden of Eden, creation saw the likeness of God there. They saw the Creator's shadow clothed in His glory ruling and watching over earth's care. Man assisted creation to flourish and fulfill its divine purpose to glorify God. They were rulers mantled with light, love, and purpose.

Our original design is to assist creation to flourish and glorify God. It is our ruling assignment as kings and priests. This includes the land and all life activities on the land. In Genesis chapter 2, it says that God had put seed in the ground *but it couldn't prosper* because there was no rain and no one to till the ground. God took care of the rain issue by causing a mist to rise and water the land. He took care of the labor issue by creating humanity in His likeness.

Since God is described in Scripture as a divine gardener (Gen. 2:8), it is no surprise that we are gardeners, too. We are earth's gardeners with divine authority. This is more than just growing vegetables in our backyards. It includes prospering the land *and* all activities on the land that impact every form of life.

MANKIND'S CREATION MANDATE

In Genesis 2:15, the word **cultivate** (Heb. *abad*) means: *to serve, to labor, to worship.* The word **keep** (Heb. *samar*) means: *to protect, watch over, and to save life.*

Here's what that meant for Adam (male and female) and for us today:

1. Father put Adam in a *specific place* to make it *fruitful.*

2. Adam's *service to the life within his territory* was part of his *worship* to God.

3. Adam's service included being a *watchman* and *protector of life.*

Mankind's assignment from the Father was to care for the seeds of divine purpose within his assigned territory. An assigned territory is an assigned *jurisdiction.* Adam was his Father's shadow and worshiped Him by causing the earth to prosper. This included the family mandate – of multiplying the image of God on earth. It meant cultivating and protecting their own seed to prosper.

Adam had ruling authority over all living things (land, sea, and air) to protect and prosper earth's destiny. Adam's bride was to help him in this divine purpose with ruling authority, too (Gen. 1:26). It was a mandate to fill the earth with God's glory.

The first Adam, male and female, were what we call a theological foreshadow of Christ (the Last Adam) and His Bride (the Church).

The command to protect was a warning that a *predator existed.* The nature of a predator is to devour life. Father didn't give Adam a task without sufficient understanding or means to fulfill his calling *and* Eden's *destiny*. He had everything he needed!

What on earth could go wrong?

THE PREDATOR

It's hard to imagine that God has an enemy. He is pure goodness. When I think of all that He has done for this world, I am floored at how some spirit beings and humans can hate and oppose Him so much. But they do.

In fact, it was one of the most gifted of His angelic princes, Lucifer, who turned on Him. Ezekiel 28 describes Lucifer as being filled with the sounds of worship, skilled in trade, full of wisdom and perfect in beauty ... until he became enamored with himself.

His heart was consumed with pride, and his own brilliance corrupted his wisdom. This inspired his evil rebellion against God, wanting to exalt himself above his Creator. Having been cast out of heaven, he wanted man's place to rule the earth. But God never gave Lucifer that role or authority.

So Lucifer (whose name means: *shining one*) became Satan (meaning: the adversary). He became the ruler of another kingdom – the kingdom of darkness.

Satan set in motion a cunning plan to trick earth's rulers to obey his voice, and break their bond with God. Doing so would incur their death and loss of governing ability. They would lose their true identity as light-bearers, allowing God's enemy to grasp the governance of earth.

Mankind's shift in his alignment would give Satan access to human activities from generation to generation for building his kingdom of darkness here.

Since earth was made for man to rule, spirit beings only have entrance and influence on earth through man's invitation or agreement. God has designed that nothing happens on earth unless a human allows it.

Having gained Adam's obedience, Satan also gleaned man's worship as *he* became earth's god and ruler. Adam should have subjugated the serpent, but he didn't. This altered the destiny of his life, family, assigned territory, and all of humanity. He lost his identity, purpose, and his authority. He lost his mantle of glory.

> WE EITHER SUBJUGATE THE ENEMY, OR THE ENEMY WILL SUBJUGATE US!

"We do not wrestle against flesh and blood but against principalities, against powers, against the rulers of darkness of this age, against spiritual hosts of wickedness in heavenly places." – Ephesians 6:12

We either subjugate the enemy, or the enemy will subjugate us! This is why we *must* rule with the authority God has given us in Christ.

As God's chosen rulers, you and I are a threat to Satan's dominion on earth. The devil continues to subjugate mankind through one simple trick – **to alter how we *think* about God, who we are, and why we are here.**

The subjugation of mankind is imperative to Satan's rule.

His trickery began with deceiving the woman – the bride. He convinced her that she didn't have sufficiency in who she was or God's intentions towards her – that God couldn't be trusted, and what God said not to eat was really a benefit to her.

So she ate it. She believed the lie and did what God said not to do. She then gave the fruit to the first Adam who also ate. He, too, disobeyed God, though he was not deceived.

WORDS ARE THE PREDATOR'S WEAPON

The word **serpent** (Heb. *nahash*) means: *the moving whisper, to enchant, divination.* Satan's words are intentional deception to make us doubt God and our identity with Him. For this reason, Father sent Jesus, *His Living Word of Truth,* to rescue us and His *written Word of truth* as our weapon against the serpent.

In Cindy Jacob's book, *Reformers Arise,* she explains how three predator ideologies have worked to subjugate and deceive the thinking of today's world. These include *"higher criticism"* (creating doubt in the inerrancy of God's Word), **Darwinism** (creating doubt in God's existence at all), and **Marxism** (which denies the role of God on earth, and so promotes government as god, parent, and educator of man's seed).[1]

"The thief comes only to steal and kill and destroy; I came so that they would have life, and have it abundantly." – John 10:10

Satan hates God and opposes the continuation of humanity. He is the predator who opposes life. He is the *whispering voice* behind abortion, homosexuality, gender bending, and depopulation agendas. He incites suicide, wars, and persecutions to slay mankind; he inspires fear, depression, and sickness to bind humanity's movement.

He hurls everything and anything he can to stop us. Deceive us. Slay us. Impede our advancement.

But God is greater!

REDEEMED BY THE KING OF GLORY

God's plans and assignments for mankind have never changed. He will bring to fulfillment what He began. The earth *will* be filled with the glory of God. The Father sent Jesus, the Last Adam, to restore what the first Adam lost – that being, our fellowship with God and our mantle of identity, purpose, and authority.

At the cross, Jesus disarmed principalities and powers, triumphing over them by the power of His atoning blood. Taking our death and curse upon Himself, HE SUBJUGATED THEM under His rule. This includes subjugating them through us, as His Body. It's why He said, *"I give you authority!"* (Luke 10:19). He also gave us power through the Holy Spirit (Acts 1:8).

Through Jesus' resurrection and ascension, we are made alive and are now seated with Him in heavenly places. Salvation in Christ is not only a return to fellowship with God, but a restored mantle of authority and anointing to prosper and protect the seeds of life and their destiny. Jesus restores in us a deep love for the Father and the world around us. Selah.

As the sons and daughters of God we must awaken and arise to our full calling. As the Bride of Christ, we must engage our mantle of being *bone of His bone and flesh of His flesh* – as being one with Him for the Father's purposes on earth.

OUR PART IN THE DESTINY OF SEEDS

The development and destiny of seed is the most prominent principle of God's Kingdom. Jesus taught His disciples many Kingdom principles regarding seed and harvest, including what hinders the full maturing of life and fruitfulness (Matt. 13).

This is not just about earthly crops but about the seed of God's Word and the seed of humanity. It is about the seed of the generations and the divine purpose of people's lives. It is about the destinies of nations.

Seed can refer to nature, lineage, and to people groups, including the righteous, as well as the unrighteous (whom God calls the sons of disobedience, Matthew 13). God's Word (living and written) are referred to as seed. So too is any thought, philosophy or ideology, as these carry the power of multiplication and a harvest.

Seed is God's concern because He is focused on a harvest of sons and daughters, and of nations. **The nurturing and protection of seed is our divine assignment**. This includes the seed and purpose of God's Word in us, our children, and the world around us.

It involves the seed of God's Word and purpose for government, education, family, media, business, and the arts and entertainment that influences society.

> THE NURTURING AND PROTECTION OF SEED IS OUR DIVINE ASSIGNMENT.

Remember, God's desire is to cover the earth with His glory; that means that He wants the cultures of nations to thrive with His glory.

When Jesus said we are to disciple nations, He meant we are to nurture the seed of God's life-giving purposes in our families and regions. It means being watchmen of our cities, state, and nation against predators.

The predators of divine purpose are evil spirits working through people and corrupt ideologies. Our call to *cultivate* and *keep* means serving our regions through intercession and involvement in every area as part of our worship of God.

Right now, the adversary is devouring our nation, and especially the children, with demonic cultural agendas. We must *shadow* Father in what He is doing about it. He is moving – He is not indifferent to what is happening in America.

The nations are in chaos. We are being called by the Prince of Peace and Ruler of the nations to rise and rule with Him regarding the well-being of this generation, and those to follow.

In this hour of history, seeds of destiny are hanging in the balance. The harvest needs OUR hands, our focus, our attention, our service and our labor. The harvest needs our worship of God, rather than an alignment with the serpent. The harvest needs our intercession and vigilance with action. We must put away all excuses and hindrances that would hinder our movement to labor with Jesus.

Serving and protecting life and land for God's purposes is an act of worship.

MOVING WITH JESUS, THE SERPENT-HEAD CRUSHER

God's response to Adam's failure in the Garden of Eden was a promise to Eve that a Seed would come through her line and crush the *head of the serpent*. A head refers to words and authority. In this case, God was referring to Satan's words and illegitimate authority.

The Promised Seed referred to Jesus who would defeat Satan's hold on earth. The Promised Seed would restore a new lineage of *image-bearers* and *light-bearers* on earth – those born of earth *and* from above.

When Jesus, the Last Adam, came He too was met by the serpent. But rather than disobeying the Father, He loved His Abba Father by refuting the predator's temptation. His work on the cross crushed *the serpent's head*.

Our identity and purpose are centered in a love bond with God in a fellowship that advances His desire to cover the earth with His glory. It is an intimate fellowship with the Father, Son, and Holy Spirit that moves us to crush the adversary's operations in our lives, homes, and regions. It means crushing the serpent's words and works of darkness wherever they are – in our government, our children's education, our family relationships, media, business practices, and entertainments.

How do we do that? By loving Him with all our heart, soul, mind, and strength. He will teach us what we are to do as we listen to Him and shadow His movement.

Earth was not created for Satan, nor are we to be the serpent's prey. **Each of us has a mission here because of who God created us to be as His sons and daughters.** Earth was created for God's glory, and so were we.

The actions of Adam and Eve were self-gratifying. All the action of the Last Adam was selfless love for the world. The actions of His Bride will be *"and they overcame him by the blood of the Lamb and the word of their testimony, and they loved not their lives even unto death." (Rev. 12:11)*

Creation is longing for Father's *shadows* to appear – the sons and daughters who **worship, work, and war for the destiny of God's purposes** in lives and nations.

You and I have been given everything we need for life and godliness. We have been given the highest rank of creation to work with Father as His delegated authority. He is calling us to step fully into our true identity and purpose in Him.

"Do not lie to one another, since you stripped off the old self with its evil practices, and have put on the new self, which is being renewed to a true knowledge according to the image of the One who created it." – Colossians 3:9-10

Pray with me: Father, teach me to walk closely with You and to put my hands to the labor You have for me. Teach me to serve my family and community as part of my worship of You – doing what You show me to do for the prosperity of life and land. In Jesus' name. Amen.

To Ponder:

- *How would you describe your identity and purpose?*
- *What is the seed God wants you to nourish and protect besides your own life?*
- *Is there an area where you need to subjugate the serpent?*

3

Occupy 'til Jesus Comes

"Occupy until I come." – Luke 19:13

I was eleven years old when my family came into a deeper experience with God called the baptism of the Holy Spirit. It was 1969 in a time known as the Charismatic Renewal and the Jesus People Movement. A lot of our songs centered on the return of Jesus. I can still hear the sound of Big John Hall's deep voice bellowing out *the King is coming!* Everyone was excited. I was concerned … *would I be ready?*

Our local church held a weekly class on evangelism – I can still recall the vivid green cover of the book we used. However, as time passed and the Lord delayed, evangelism began to wane and many went back to life as usual.

Like Peter, much of the Church went back to fishing, but not for the souls of humanity.

And so we slept.

It seems to be a human thing we do whenever God tarries. But Jesus said we are to *"occupy"* until He comes, not sleep! Not be distracted.

The King is still coming and He will reign on earth. Meanwhile, however, we have a work to do. We must wake up, rise up, throw off a slumbering spirit and step into our identity and purpose. We must get back to fishing for souls and governing nations, now more than ever!

Jesus, the *Man of Fire* who sits on the throne of heaven, is calling for a Bride who is *on fire* and moving with Him for the nations. While we slept, the tares have matured and the enemy is trafficking the nations in evil.

When Jesus said to "occupy" until He comes, it was a charge told through a parable about a nobleman and his servants (Luke 19:11-27). To *"occupy"* means: *to carry on a business, especially in matters of trade for increasing wealth.* It is an *action* word. The "occupation" in this context was linked to increasing the wealth of an estate belonging to a nobleman (a man of noble birth, a lord).

JESUS, THE MAN OF FIRE, IS CALLING FOR A BRIDE WHO IS ON FIRE AND MOVING WITH HIM FOR THE NATIONS.

In this parable, Jesus told of a lord who was called away to be crowned king but would then return. To make sure his interests were well cared for during his absence, he selected ten servants to carry on his business. He gave each one a talent (a measure of currency) for trading. After the nobleman left on his journey, the *citizens* of the land rose up and declared, *"We will not have him as our king!"* They then sent a delegation to tell him so.

Upon the nobleman's return, the servants gave account of what they had done with the talent they'd been given to carry on his business. Nine servants multiplied their money for advancing the lord's interests (who was also now king). They prospered his estate and were *rewarded with governing authority over cities.* Their faithfulness was a sign of honoring his decree and desires.

One servant, however, hid his talent. He did nothing to advance the king's affairs. The king called the servant wicked and took away what he had been given. And lastly, the citizens who refused the king's reign were taken away and slain.

Obviously, Jesus was speaking about Himself through this parable. In His years on earth, He was Man of highest noble birth. He was recognized by His followers as the Lord, doing the business of His Father with the wealth of heaven. Through this parable, He was letting His disciples know that soon He would be leaving to receive His crown and Kingdom. He is both Lord and King. In His absence, His disciples would be given currency with which to steward and increase His interests. They were to multiply what He gave them and increase His Kingdom on earth. (Selah)

The terms that Jesus used in the story were intentional and involved finances, business, and citizenry. The word **citizens** (Grk. *polites*) referred to the inhabitants of a *city-state (polis).* A *city-state* includes its boundaries, activities within its borders, as well as its governing policies. The term *polis* is the same root for both *citizens (polites)* and a city-state's *politics (politika); politics* refers to the affairs of the city and all activities associated with the functioning of its governing policies (power structures).

In ancient Greek culture the life of *citizens* and the affairs of *state* and *politics* were intertwined. In other words, personal, social, and political life went hand in hand.[1] America, too, was founded on the same principle. The United States is a republic established on a constitution of the people, by the people, and for the people. As citizens, we are tasked to be involved in the affairs of state and governing policies.

Okay, back to the story. Jesus was letting His disciples know that the increase of His Kingdom included personal, social and governing policies of regions. This was seen in the reward given for faithfulness – **the reward of ruling cities!**

Interestingly, Jesus spoke of the citizens who didn't mind the nobleman's role of being lord of a territory, but when it came to him being crowned over everything ... oh my! No, we will not have this! We will not have him involved in our social activities, state affairs, or politics. THAT would be going way too far!

OUR ROLE IS TO BE A VOICE FOR JESUS' GOVERNMENT AND PRESENCE IN ALL REALMS OF LIFE AND SOCIETY.

In today's world we know it as *keep your faith to yourself! Separation of Church and state!* Jesus can be Lord of someone's life, but don't let HIS policies influence social policies!

However, as servants and ambassadors of the Lord Jesus Christ, our role has always been to be a voice for His government and presence in all realms of life and society. He has chosen to govern through us for the well-being of the generations. This is not about tyranny, but about prospering life.

THE OCCUPATION OF FAITH

Jesus used many parables to explain His Kingdom. In this one, it was the principle of faithfulness in trade and finances for advancing His Kingdom. Trade is an exchange of goods or currency by which increase is made, needs are met, and desires are fulfilled. Exchange is a key concept in Father's Kingdom. The cross itself was a divine exchange for Kingdom advancement – Jesus' life for our debt. In return He gained the whole world.

In this parable, it was the Lord's *measure of currency* (talent) that was given to the servants. So what is the currency we have been given to advance Jesus' Kingdom?

The most direct meaning of talent here is money. What are we doing with our finances to advance God's Kingdom? Anything?

Scripture also speaks of the *riches of His grace and glory* being given us. The King's glory is the realm of His throne (authority and power), His fire, His angels, and worship. It's the realm of His decrees, manifold wisdom and revelation, and more. It's where all needs are supplied. *The King gives us what we need for what we are to do.*

The term *riches of His grace* speaks of the divine favor and ability given us to receive what we need. We are to engage His unlimited wealth for prospering His interests in our lives and in the earth.

Scripture says we have also been given the *measure of faith* (Rom. 12:3). Faith is said to be the *currency* of heaven – it is a spiritual frequency that effects change. Faith opens the way for God's Kingdom to manifest on earth.

You can have a lot of faith or a little faith. You can also grow what measure you have. In God's Kingdom nothing happens without faith. Kingdom riches are accessed and prospered through faith. Every word we hear from God must be joined with faith for it to be *profitable* in our lives and Kingdom assignments.

> YOU CAN HAVE A LOT OF FAITH, OR A LITTLE FAITH. YOU CAN ALSO GROW WHAT MEASURE YOU HAVE.

To occupy territory and advance the King's purposes on earth requires the active movement of faith. The measure given us is for Kingdom works and His rule of light over darkness. In this hour, God is bringing His people into new levels of faith for releasing His Kingdom in greater measure.

As God's sons and daughters, we are also given unique gifts and abilities for Kingdom purposes. We are given words and promises. Faith is to be mixed with each of these to increase the

King's *business* (*occupation*) in the land – including in government, education, family, media, arts and entertainment. We will look more at those in the chapters ahead.

The nations are His business and we must learn to occupy the public square and replace corruption with what promotes life and goodness.

Faith releases the grace and anointing of God for Kingdom increase in our lives. It empowers spiritual growth and divine ability to minister to the world around us.

When Jesus selected *ten* servants it wasn't random. In mathematics, numbers are based on the **power of ten**. Ten is a *power multiplier*. In biblical numerology, ten speaks of God's perfect order and a completed cycle. In Genesis chapter 1, the phrase "*and God said*" is listed ten times – each time bringing something new into manifestation.

In Scripture, the number ten is linked to supernatural creativity, ruling, judgment, and deliverance. It speaks of old cycles ending and new ones beginning. It is linked with cleansing, worship, and divine instruction for advancing God's purposes in the earth.

In the Hebrew language, ten is represented by the letter *Yod* and is symbolized by a hand, signifying **strength and work**. As we saw in the story of the nobleman-king, nine servants put their hands to the work of his kingdom, but one didn't. That nobleman knew there was a new order coming and he was establishing his power multiplier of ten to bring in a new order of kingdom increase. Nevertheless, as in this story, we all have a choice, even as Christ's servants. But with choice also comes reward or punishment.

Evil has risen worldwide, and as believers we are now in an *all-hands-on deck* hour! The King is calling us to do something with what we have been given. He is coming back and His justice and judgment will be seen in the earth. In truth, it is already being displayed. He is here. He is involved. May we engage the faith and grace given us and not hide our light ... or refute His rule.

James 2:26 tells us that *living* faith has *living* works. Faith without corresponding works is a dead faith. The one who did not increase what he had been given, had no faith for increase. Works do not save us, or gain us acceptance with God, but we were created to do good works – His works.

We were created for increase!

No wonder Jesus told His disciples time and again, *"Where is your faith?"* He had great works for them to do. He wanted them to experience continual Kingdom increase in their lives and ministries. It's the same for you – He wants you to experience Kingdom increase in your life, business, and His ministry through you.

> LIVING FAITH HAS LIVING WORKS.

Author Joyce Meyers once said, "God will never hold you responsible for the gifts He did not give you." This is true, yet I will add that He *will* hold us responsible for the measure He *has* given us.

"To whom much is given, much shall be required" (Luke 12:48).

RULING: FROM GENESIS TO REVELATION

From beginning to end, God's Word is a story of worship, work, and governing. From Eden to Joshua to the eternal rule of the saints, man's call is to rule over the works of Father's hands. He is a good Father who wants His children working with Him, and so delegates His authority to us.

Much of the American Church has lost this understanding. We must now gain it back.

When Jesus came, He gave His disciples authority and commanded them to not only heal the sick, cleanse the lepers, raise the dead, and cast out devils, but to preach the Kingdom and *disciple nations* (Matt. 10:8; Luke 9:2). At the coming of Christ, we will be assigned cities to govern. We are learning how to do it now as He teaches us to worship and war for life and the land.

FROM BEGINNING TO END, GOD'S WORD IS A STORY OF WORSHIP, WORK, AND GOVERNING.

It is ill imagined that we can be choose to be unfaithful regarding our calling now and then expect to rule later. We are defining our destiny with our daily choices to either believe God and do what He says, or not.

YOU ARE AN AMBASSADOR

Faithfulness with the measure we have been given positions us for specific Kingdom operations. When Paul called himself an *ambassador of the Lord,*[2] he understood his call as being the King's delegate – one sent from the Throne Room to care for the King's interests on earth. An ambassador has the sending government's authority and provision for the work they are to do in the foreign land where they are sent.

The realms of spiritual authority for ruling that we have been called to walk in as Christians requires a mindset of authority that has not been well-taught (if taught at all) in many Christians' experience. It is imperative in this hour to put on Christ in a fuller way – Christ, who is the love of God *and* the Lord of armies.

We, too, are ambassadors (emissaries) caring for the King's interests on earth. We have His backing and provision for the work we are to do in filling all things with His Kingdom presence. When people come to my office for inner healing and deliverance ministry, the Lord has taught me to see them as ambassadors trapped by the enemy. I don't think of them so much as broken people, though they may carry a broken heart. I think of them as ambassadors who need divine assistance where they've been wounded, and help in breaking free of Satan's entrapments. The goal, however doesn't end with healing and freedom, but is something needed so they can carry on the work God has called them to do.

YOU HAVE AN APOSTOLIC MISSION

Are you now getting a bigger scope of how much God's Word involves your call to govern? Here is another ruling concept in Scripture: as ambassadors, we are an apostolic people carrying an *apostolic mission* to transform regions with the King's culture, the King's desires, and the King's good will. It's why Jesus gave the Church the equipping ministry of the apostle (Eph. 4:11).

The ancient Greek meaning of an *"apostle"* is *sent one*. It referred to generals who not only conquered regions, but established the culture of the government they represented. Today's apostles train God's people to establish heaven's culture in their regions as part of the believer's ministry.

Over the past century, God has been restoring the fullness of the five-fold gifts of apostle, prophet, evangelist, pastor, and teacher (Eph. 4). Since the fourth century, when Roman Emperor Constantine instituted a state Church, four of the five equipping gifts became largely inoperative. Those four were the apostle, prophet, evangelist and teacher.

> AS AN APOSTOLIC PEOPLE, WE ARE SENT TO BRING THE CULTURE OF HEAVEN TO EARTH.

Under Constantine, the Church was removed from the foundation of the apostles and prophets and restructured with many false doctrines. **This left the Church untaught, unskilled, and largely ineffective in her true calling.**

She was made to survive on just one equipping gift, and that was the pastor who was left to try and do it all! Thank God for pastors who have been faithful to their calling, and thank God for His restoration of the rest of Jesus' equipping team!

It is the apostolic and prophetic ministry that shifts us from passivity and self-focus to Kingdom movement. This is where the Church is at now. We are in a transition era that is changing the face of the Church. What was lost is being restored so that we can now move as an apostolic, prophetic, evangelistic, shepherding and discipling company.

As an apostolic people, we are sent to bring the culture of heaven to earth. When Israel was commanded to possess Canaan, it meant driving out the presence of principalities and demon gods. It meant destroying the altars that invited their presence. These principalities demanded child sacrifice and rituals of sorcery and sexual immorality. These practices empowered demonic activity in the region and kept the people and land in spiritual bondage.

If you look around, it is a picture of nations today. People who are aligned with evil are driving evil ideologies that are destroying the minds and bodies of men, women, and children, driving corrupt laws, promoting lawlessness, and suppressing truth and the people from prospering.

BREAKING TERRITORIAL STRONGHOLDS

In the Old Testament, we see that Israel's battles weren't just natural ones but spiritual ones. God's anger towards the ancient Canaanites was because of their alignment with iniquitous acts and demon principalities that destroyed life and opposed God. They worshipped wickedness in high places that defiled mankind and killed children. The cup of iniquity was full and God took action. God pays attention to the earth that belongs to

Him. He pays attention to who sides with Him and who opposes Him.

It is the same warfare we are facing in the world today.

In ancient times God had His part to do, but so did Israel. God repeatedly spoke of His part that He would *"expel, dispossess, send away, annihilate, thrust out, drive out, destroy, exterminate, and cut off"* the enemy activity defiling the land and lives. Israel's part was to possess the land as they followed God's leading in every place.[3] While God worked, they also warred.

Removing demonic activity from the land was a divine command. To not do so was a sin in God's eyes.[4]

Today, our Kingdom warfare isn't with natural swords but with intercession *and* active involvement to dispossess evil *and* implement God's goodness. We have our part to take down evil works and bind territorial spirits that destroy the destinies of lives and nations ... we must move especially on behalf of the children!

> WE ARE TO PREACH THE KINGDOM OF GOD AND DISCIPLE CULTURE IN RIGHTEOUSNESS.

Evil operates through wicked spirits, philosophies and ungodly societal activities. We are to preach the Kingdom of God *and* disciple spheres of culture in righteousness. To do so is an act of love.

When the light is absent from culture it creates a spiritual vacuum that darkness is eager to fill.

Many Christians are not "occupying until He comes" for many reasons, including two common false beliefs:

False belief #1: "The anti-Christ is going to take over anyway so there is no point to resist." This fear-driven doctrine exalts the power of the anti-Christ over the power of Christ, and the only hope seen is in being raptured soon. People with this perspective see no purpose for engaging cultural change since it will all be burned up anyway. Or, Jesus will make it all right when He comes back. Either way, it's not our problem and we are just going to bunker down in our personal faith while nations go to hell. It is a faithless, hopeless mentality that prevents us from taking our position as His faithful witnesses who love not our lives, even unto death.

False belief #2: "Jesus wasn't political so the Church shouldn't be involved in politics – our role is only a spiritual one; besides, you can't legislate righteousness." So, legislating wickedness is okay? Legislating abortion, pedophilia, racism and persecution are okay? Jesus' servants should always be involved in all aspects of the *polis* and the policies that impact them. Righteous legislation isn't about forcing religion on others, it IS about prospering and protecting lives from life destroying laws and evil practices. It's about healing culture. Remember the *cultivate* and *keep* mandate?

A World in Need of Healing

In December, 2021, Google came out with a publication called, "Year in Search." The publication was about the word most "googled" on the internet in 2021. That word was "healing." It included physical healing, social healing, relational healing and emotional healing.

Today's world has sent out a cry for healing, and we are the Body of the Healer. Should we not be involved in every aspect of a culture crying for healing?

Remember, we are caring for the well-being of HIS earth and the people on it.

Long ago, God promised to bless Abraham saying that in him all the families of the earth would be blessed (Gen. 12:3). That blessing is in Jesus – the son of Abraham (Matt. 1:1). We are His

Body to carry that blessing into all the earth. As the curse has been removed from us through Christ's blood, so must we move to break the curse off the land. The earth is waiting for us!

The Genesis 1:26 mandate has not ended. God's plans have not changed. We are caretakers of the earth wherever Father places us.

> WE ARE CARETAKERS OF THE EARTH, WHEREVER FATHER PLACES US.

This is who we are as the sons and daughters of God – removing what destroys life and establishing what promotes life. It is who we are as the light and those who carry His glory.

YOU ARE THE SALT OF THE EARTH

Jesus said, *"You are the salt of the earth. But if the salt loses its taste, how shall its saltiness be restored? It is no longer good for anything except to be thrown out and trampled under people's feet"* (Matt. 5:13 ESV). Good salt carries a bold flavor, enhances food, and makes a more delightful experience. It brings out the good. Salt also preserves food from corruption.

People are meant to experience the delight of God. We are here to release the rich flavor of His goodness *and* to preserve culture from decay. Right now, every system of American society is in a state of corruption and decay from government to education to media, family and business. Please pass the salt!

We need salt in our legislation halls, school curriculums, and marriage relationships. We need salt in media and business practices. We need salt in our arts and entertainment industries.

Unfortunately, too much of the Church has lost its savor. It has been passive rather than bold. It has been slack in preserving culture from corruption. A savorless Church is one that is trodden underfoot by men. We were not saved to be trodden underfoot, but to tread the enemy!

"Behold, I have given you the authority to tread on serpents and scorpions, and over all the power of the enemy, and nothing shall hurt you." – Jesus (Luke 10:19 ESV)

Your presence in this world is so significant. **By now I hope you are seeing the vastness of your call to be a world changer as Jesus' Body.**

We are the salt sent of God to bring healing. We are the light that must radiate *beyond ourselves* for breaking strongholds of corruption wherever we find them.

Pray with me: *Father, help me to rise with the Spirit of faith to do the works You have called me to do! Send me to help break my region free of corruption. Teach me to tread over the works of darkness and not be silent, that Your works be accomplished through me. In Jesus' name. Amen.*

To Ponder:

- *How does God want you to be salt in culture?*
- *Where do you want to see corruption ended? What are you going to do about it?*
- *How are you using your money to advance Kingdom purposes?*

4

STANDING AT THE GATES
WITH JESUS

*"...upon this rock I will build My Church [Ekklesia]; and the gates of
Hades will not prevail [be superior in strength] against it. I will
give you the keys of the kingdom of heaven; and whatever you bind on
earth shall have been bound in heaven, and whatever you loose on
earth shall have been loosed in heaven."*
Matthew 16:18-19

One day, Jesus took His disciples to a place called the
gates of Hades (or gates of Hell). That gate was a cave
situated at the foot of Mount Hermon. The people of
the region believed it to be a gateway to the
underworld. In ancient Greek religion, Hades was known as the
god of the dead and king of the underworld. According to the
book of Enoch, Mt. Hermon was the place where 120 *Watchers*

(angels) descended (leaving their *"proper abode"*) and took the *daughters of men* as wives. It was a direct rebellion against **Yahweh** (the **LORD**; see Gen. 6; James 1:6). The offspring of this mixed breed were giants known as the Nephilim.[1]

Yahweh (sometimes translated as *Jehovah, or LORD*) is God's *personal* name used over 6800 times in Scripture. It is associated with His sovereignty, limitlessness, and delivering power as the God who answers by fire and whose name is to be remembered from generation to generation (Ex. 3:13-15; 1 Kings 18:24).[2]

Jesus' Hebrew name, **Yeshua,** means: **Yahweh is salvation**. Yeshua came bearing His Father's name (John 5:43); it was a declaration that Yahweh owned the earth, not other gods, and Yahweh's Son was here to deliver it from sin and evil.

This place, labeled as the gates of Hades, was also where the headwaters of the Jordan River flowed out. Every spring, the melted snow of Mt. Hermon would flow out of the mouth of the cave to water the land. People there believed that the *fertility gods* who rested during the winter came out with the water to bring new life. People would come to the gates of Hades bringing offerings and rituals to entice the gods to release their blessing of water from the underworld. These rituals included child sacrifice, sexual orgies, acts of bestiality, and the practice of homosexuality.

Just outside the cave stood the temple of Pan (known as the Panion or Panium). Pan was known as a powerful god of fertility and was depicted as half man, half goat (otherwise known as the *goat god*, or *Baphomet*). Pan was the personification of perversion and the sexual powers of Lucifer and his music.[3]

The region of Mount Hermon was a major center for Baal worship and was said to be *established on the "rock of Pan."* Bible scholars believe that it was there on Mt. Hermon where Jesus was transfigured in His meeting with Moses and Elijah. It is also said that this act symbolized Jesus' declared intent to reclaim His Father's purposes with mankind and overturn what Lucifer and the Watchers had done in defiling God's image-bearers.

Jesus' Church would be built, not on the rock of Pan, but on the rock of *Christ, the Anointed One* – **the Son of Yahweh who was mantled to restore earth to original design.** Such a declaration would strike to the very heart of Satan's works.

Growing up in Western Christianity, I was taught that Greek gods were simply myths, but they weren't. They were ruling principalities and powers as realities that both Old and New Testament fathers of the faith very well understood. They are still spiritual realities at work today.

UNDERSTANDING SPIRITUAL GATEWAYS

The significance of Jesus taking His disciples to that place is vast in its meaning for us now. He was making it clear that His Kingdom was coming in power and authority – through His *Church, HIS* worshipers – to bind the enemy's access and activity in the earth.

Jesus' *Church* (Grk. *Ekklesia*) would stand on the rock of the revelation of Him as the Son of God. They would restore true worship of the Creator and bring true life back to regions.

> JESUS' CHURCH IS BUILT ON THE ROCK OF CHRIST – THE SON OF YAHWEH WHO IS MANTLED TO RESTORE EARTH TO ORIGINAL DESIGN.

Through the ages, mountains have been viewed as the *dwelling place of gods* and where spiritual encounters take place. Scripture itself shows us a direct link between earthly mountains, spiritual portals (or gateways), and man's worship. God established this and Satan copied it (as at Mt. Hermon). Everything Satan does is a counterfeit to God's designs.

Eden, where Adam met with God, was not only a garden but a mountain too (Eze. 28:12-19). Moses met with God on Mt. Sinai where he was given the **blueprint for worship** in the form of the Tabernacle (later erected as the Temple on Mt. Zion). That blueprint of divine worship was in the **pattern of the cross**. In the Old Testament, the Tabernacle was the habitation of God's glory in the midst of His people. It reflected God's covenant with Israel and His glory that gave them victory over every enemy. They were glory-carriers. Every detail of the Tabernacle was a prophetic picture of Jesus, the King of Glory, and the realms of spiritual access He would open to everyone by His work on the cross.

Because of Jesus' shed blood and resurrection, we are now the living temple of God, linked to the heavenly Mt. Zion where we are seated with Christ in heavenly places (Heb. 12:22-24).

All worship involves sacrifices that either invite the presence and glory of God, or the presence of demons depending on who is being worshipped through those sacrifices. The gates of Hades was a place where evil forces were *hosted* through rituals that invoked evil activity.

The idolatrous worship at the gates of Hades connected the region both to the gods of the underworld and to evil principalities inhabiting the high places on Mt. Hermon (remember, spirits can only operate where mankind gives them permission to do so, whether through our ignorance or intention).

When Jesus decreed the authority of His Church to *"bind and loose"* it was not just for that place alone, but for every place where demonic activity has been established on earth.

Someone else may open evil portals, but Jesus' Ekklesia has the authority and keys to close the door and lock it!

PRINCIPALITIES AND MOUNTAINS

Spiritual portals that impact regions and nations are most powerful when established at a mountain because of a mountain's prominence. Mountains are high places and places of refuge or stronghold (whether for good or evil). Mountains are not just the natural ones of a geographical landscape, but can also speak of what we refer to as the *mountains of culture* or *influence*, such as **government, education, business, and media** (more on this in a moment).

These "cultural mountains" hold a dominant presence of social influence. Wicked forces seek places of influence to control social mindsets and release wicked activity.

Nations today are battling principalities, ruling powers, and wickedness in high places in a way never seen before. This is because these have been invited into human affairs through ungodly worship practices, including Satanic blood sacrifices, murder and abortion, witchcraft, and sexual immorality. This generation is being trained to open evil portals through games, movies and books. Many government officials around the world have learned the power of the supernatural and are opening all kinds of ungodly portals through wicked practices. This power manifests as tyranny and cultural bondage.

Nahum 3:4 describes these activities as how *Satan sells (trafficks) nations through whoredoms and families through witchcraft.* Satan understands the principle of trade that I discussed in Chapter 3. He, too, is a *trader* who increases his kingdom through human activity.

GATEWAY LOCATIONS

In Matthew 16, the Greek word for *gate* (*pyle*) means: a *gateway into a city*, a *palace*, a *temple*, a *prison*, or *access into any state.* In ancient Hebrew culture, city gates were designated places where legal transactions, trade agreements, and judicial sentences were made. It was a point of access into the city. Temples dedicated to gods created a portal for those gods. This spiritual dynamic is the same today.

Spiritual gates and portals can be opened anywhere, though certain places are more strategic than others for a greater social impact. *Altars of worship* established at a geographical border, government house, designated temple, or gathering can establish either the presence of God or demonic activity in that place or region.

Businesses that serve demonic agendas through their goods, services and practices can release evil into culture. Government officials who make sacrifices to demons to gain power and favor open an evil gateway into their jurisdictions. Yes, there are officials who do that. It's why it's important who we vote for, from local elections to national ones.

The opposite is also true – business and government officials can release God's glory into the land through their actions and practices.

The diagram here shows the relationship between the mountains of culture, social gateways, and man's worship. They are interconnected. Worship and the actions of

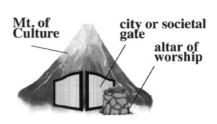

prominent influences either opens the access of God's glory, or hell's activity, into society.

Satan seeks gateways to establish his agendas in every facet of culture, especially in government, business, judicial decisions, and education. As stated, it takes human activity to open portals, whether for good or for evil.

WE ARE GATEWAYS, TOO!

There is another access point, however, into spiritual realms – the Body of Christ. We are the temple of the Holy Spirit – a gateway with access into the heavenly reams. And what's more is that we have keys to open and shut hell! It's time to use what we have been given.

Paul said, *"Don't you know that you are a temple of God and that the Spirit of God dwells in you? ... Or what agreement does the temple of God have with idols? For we are the temple of the Living God..."* (1 Cor. 3:16; 2 Cor. 6:16).

When Jesus called us His *Ekklesia* (translated as *"Church"*), he used an ancient Greek term referring to **a group of citizens called out to convene and make decisions regarding social issues, and what actions were needed.** This group legislated on legal matters that impacted society. Jesus intentionally used this term to define how His Church would function regarding even social matters.

Yes, we are called out to be involved with a voice of wisdom and spiritual authority to bind demonic powers that drive destruction in human affairs. We are to give counsel with action to free lives and land from demonic bondage.

As Yeshua's Ekklesia, we have the keys to steward life and revoke demonic entrance into the earth. How? By hosting God's presence continually. By unifying in intercession and using our voice of authority *with action* for righteousness ... by going after the manifestation of our Father's Kingdom. This is significant!

Jesus' decree at the gates of hell established the *very nature and mission of His Ekklesia* – it would be to carry His authority for *locking and unlocking spiritual realms.* **Our mission is to not only lock up evil, but release His glory to heal, restore, and deliver lives and land.**

It's time for the Church to understand our role to host God's presence on earth, steward the seeds of life and land, and shut out predators.

While the Last Adam reclaimed the authority that the first Adam had lost through sin, it is the Body of the Last Adam who are to reclaim what the first Adam failed to do as a son worshipping at the gates of his territory and binding the serpent's activity.

WATER GATES

Psalm 29:2 says to give unto the Lord the glory due HIS name. Those headwaters flowing from Mt. Hermon was a part of God's creation. Worship there should have been attributed to Him. Satan is a liar and a thief always looking to take the glory that belongs to God. Water is a key element for life, both naturally and spiritually. Trade happens on waters. Evil spirits not only inhabit places on land, but in waterways, too. They are called water spirits, such as Leviathan.[4] Reclaiming territories includes restoring the worship of Yahweh on the waters (Ps. 89:25).

The fact that John the Baptist was sent to baptize people in repentance in the waters of the Jordan that flowed from Mt. Hermon signified the power of God's Kingdom as greater than the forces of Satan's agendas. God can redeem anything! His purpose is to redeem everything!

STANDING AT THE GATES WITH FATHER

"Behold, children are a gift (inheritance) of the Lord, the fruit of the womb is a reward. Like arrows in the hand of a warrior, so are the children of one's youth. Blessed is the man whose quiver is full of them; they will not be ashamed [disappointed] when they contend with their enemies in the gate." (Ps. 127:3-5, NLT)

To stand at the gates with Jesus is to also stand there with Abba Father and Holy Spirit. Our life with Christ is neither a passive nor a solitary one.

The Scripture above paints a powerful picture of a warrior father whose children are like arrows in his quiver. Arrows are weapons of war. This warrior father isn't standing alone, but he is there with his children, his arrows, contending with his enemies *at the gate!* And look! He is not disappointed! Why? Because his *shadows* are standing with him.

Our Father is a Man of War who contends for what belongs to Him ... namely, everything! We stand with Him against the enemy's access, influence, and rule. The Hebrew word here for **contend** (*dabar*) means: **to speak, answer, subdue, command, destroy, declare, teach.** **It is speech that carries authority.**

> *"These are the things which you shall do: **speak** the truth to one another; **judge** with truth and judgment for peace at your gates. Also let none of you devise evil in your heart against another, and do not love perjury (lying). For all these things are what I hate!"*
> (Zech. 8:16-17)

Practically speaking, this means we don't stand idly by watching the enemy plunder our resources, indoctrinate our children in sorcery and immorality, legislate wickedness, and tyrannize society with corrupt government mandates. WE SAY SOMETHING! We resist the enemy. We do not comply with him.

In this passage, the Hebrew word for *gate* (*sha'ar*) means: *opening, door, port, entrance, or public place of meeting.* Gates need gatekeepers who are watchmen. Remember, Adam's first command was to be a watchman. It was part of his worship.

In society, gatekeepers include people like mayors, school superintendents, parents, newspaper publishers, judges, civil authorities, broadcast companies, movie producers, music companies, pastors, and so on. They decide what is allowed or not allowed. As the Ekklesia we are all spiritual gatekeepers wherever we are. As American citizens we are gatekeepers of our Republic. Parents are gatekeepers of their children's education and entertainment. Pastors are gatekeepers of their congregations. Apostles and prophets are gatekeepers of regions. Teachers are gatekeepers of truth.

Each of us stand as a gatekeeper in more than one place.

GATES ARE ALSO PERSONAL

Gates are more than just cultural, they are personal – the mind gate, eye gate, ear gate, and mouth gate. It also includes our reproductive gate. We are to stand with Father at these gates, too. We can't guard a city gate if we are not faithful in guarding our personal gates.

> OUR HEART BOND WITH GOD IS THE POWER BEHIND ALL GATEKEEPING

Corruption in our lives is a worship issue at our gates.

This is why the first commandment is to love the Lord with all our heart, soul, mind and strength. This heart bond with God is the power behind *all* gatekeeping.

Do we love our Father? How much do we pray? Read His Word? Obey Him? Seek His Kingdom?

Jesus said, *"If any man wants to come after Me, let him deny himself, take up his cross and follow Me."* Gatekeeping begins with picking up our cross and following Jesus, the Son of Yahweh.

As believers, we are a holy people set apart for the Lord. Our fellowship is with Him and not with idols or other gods. Stopping the devil's access into culture begins by refusing his access into our own lives.

LET THE KING OF GLORY IN!

"Lift up your heads, you gates, and be lifted up you ancient doors, that the King of Glory may come in. Who is this King of Glory? The Lord strong and mighty, the Lord mighty in battle." (Ps. 24:7-8)

Jesus is the King of Glory who stands at the gates waiting to be welcomed into our regions. Will we let Him in? Or will we let principalities in? Will we contend with the enemy? Or will we allow the waters of wickedness to flood our regions?

The enemy has established himself at the gates of American culture while the Father's light-bearers have too often stood silent. Evil that has entered through our cultural gates includes:

- Abortion
- Human trafficking
- Unprotected borders
- Compromised election system
- Corrupt laws and judges
- Corrupt medical practices
- Corruption in education
- Suppression of free speech
- Suppression of religious freedom
- Government waste and misuse of public finances
- Suppression of truth

These are just a few of what we are aware of most.

Knowing the problem, however, isn't enough. We are to pray and take action with divine solutions. We must labor with the King to subdue evil and release His glory for the sake of the people, especially the children!

At the time of this writing, millions of Americans realize the corruption our government has become but don't know what to do. Many who have come from communist nations seeking freedom from failed governments and tyranny are deeply concerned about where America stands. They say that our current cultural path parallels the revolutions of Mao Zedong, Joseph Stalin, Adolph Hitler, Fidel Castro, and Nicolas Maduro Moros under whose regimes millions died.

As God's people we must move to speak up for life and liberty.

We must wake up! Show up! Speak up!

If not us, who? If not now, when?

God's Word tells us to submit to God *and* resist the devil ... not submit to the devil and resist God! We are to destroy the devil's works, not tolerate them. As Yeshua's Ekklesia, *and* as national citizens, we must resist tyranny imposed by those with wicked agendas.

We have a responsibility both spiritually and from our U.S. Constitution to hold wicked leaders accountable for actions that are evil and contrary to God's laws and our constitutional rights.

Father is calling His warrior sons and daughters to rise and stand with Him now. It's harvest time, and the enemy is also at the gates of culture wanting to steal the harvest meant for God.

OPENING THE GATES FOR THE HARVEST

Jesus said to lift up our eyes and see the harvest. The harvest time is now! Millions of souls will be coming into Christ's Kingdom over the next few years through increased waves of fresh outpourings of the Holy Spirit through evangelism and revival. Another part of harvest time is the maturing of the saints. Mature spiritual fathers and mothers will be needed as the harvest comes in to help grow believers in faith and in their identity and purpose in God.

Past moves of the Spirit are merging with a fresh outpouring of the Holy Spirit to bring Christ's Body into her fulness as a Bride prepared for the King and who labors with Him.

Our commission to *"go into all the world and preach the gospel of the kingdom"* is three-fold: to *individuals*, to *communities*, and to *culture*. I encourage you to make a list of each of these areas and ask Holy Spirit to show you how He wants to increase your influence to them.

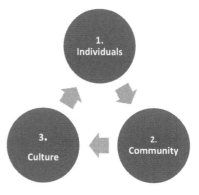

You are an important part of bringing in the harvest *and* discipling nations. Your God-given gifts are important to how your influence is expressed. We will look more at this in a later chapter.

The Holy Spirit is pouring out fresh fire to share God's love everywhere we go – to relatives, neighbors, co-workers, and with strangers to whom God prompts us to speak. That might be someone at Walmart, a waiter, or people at a PTA meeting.

The Holy Spirit is also fanning the flame of greater unity in the Body of Christ for regional spiritual awakening through evangelism. This is where churches come together – laboring with the Lord of harvest – to revive hearts with love, truth, and hope. Revival, however, must lead to cultural reformation.

THE HARVEST AND THE MOUNTAINS OF CULTURE

Reformation is where culture and social mindsets are transformed as society awakens to righteousness through God's manifest glory.

Psalm 72:3-4 (NET) says, *"The mountains will bring news of peace to the people, and the hills will announce justice. He will defend the oppressed among the people; he will deliver the children of the poor and crush the oppressor."*

In this passage, The Passion Translation translates *"mountains"* as the *"mountains of influence."* This term (*Mountains of Culture* or *Influence*) began to appear in 1988, when Loren Cunningham (founder of Youth With a Mission) was praying about how Christians could truly turn the world around for Jesus. He said a list came to mind regarding seven areas of society that are key influencers of culture that needed to be reached in order to turn the *nation* back to God.

The next day, Cunningham met with Dr. Bill Bright (then leader of Campus Crusade for Christ) and shared his list with him. Surprisingly, Bright pulled out his own list that he too had gotten in prayer on how to bring hope and change to the nation.

The two lists were amazingly similar. The seven areas they saw that needed revival *and* reformation are: **Family, Church, Education, Government, Media, Arts & Entertainment, and Commerce (Business).**[5]

We call these the *"7 Mountains of Culture or Influence."*

These areas of influence help shape the mindsets of society. They are intended by God to minister the truth of His love and goodness. Under the influence of righteous voices, they do just that; but under evil influences they bring nations to utter ruin. We are experiencing that ruin today in America because of unattended gates at these cultural mountains.

We can turn the battle at the gates by standing in prayer and speaking for truth and righteousness.

These 7 *mountains* are *gateways* through which flow the waters of ideologies – philosophies and beliefs that shape cultural mindsets and social activities. People, communities and nations operate through belief structures, whether good or evil. Whoever governs the mountains governs society.

It's not enough to have a salvation limited to our own well-being. We are to bring good news to the people from every mountain top. We must shut access to evil and open the portals of heaven.

The hour is late, and we cannot simply wish for change. We must act for change. We must speak for change.

> IT'S NOT ENOUGH TO HAVE A SALVATION LIMITED TO OUR OWN WELL-BEING.

For the sake of this generation and those to come, we must rise for revival *and* reformation. We must stop the waters of hell and open the floodgates of heaven.

A TIME TO THRESH THE MOUNTAINS

In Isaiah 41:15-16, God tells His people, *"Look, I am making you like a sharp threshing sledge [having teeth], new and double-edged. **You will thresh the mountains** and crush them; you will make the hills like straw (chaff). You will winnow them and the wind will blow them away; the wind [storm] will scatter them. You will rejoice in the Lord; you will boast in the Holy One of Israel."* (NET)

Threshing is the process of removing chaff from the grain. Chaff is the dry, lifeless structure surrounding the grain. In ancient times, this was done with an instrument having sharp "teeth." After threshing came the winnowing where the chaff and grain were thrown together into the air. As the grain fell due to its weightier substance, the wind would blow the chaff away.

We are in a new move of the Holy Spirit where He is raising His people up to be like a new, double-edged threshing instrument. That double-edge is the Word of the Lord in our mouths as we learn to move with Him to break society free of corruption. It's time to remove what is not giving life!

King Solomon said, *"A wise king winnows [scatters] the wicked, and drives the threshing wheel over them."* (Pro. 20:26)

The Hebrew word for *wicked* or *evil* (*rasha*) means: **the person of the devouring eye**. It speaks of someone who *seeks to devour life* rather than empower it. There are people whose desire is to devour life through evil legislation, corrupt education, human trafficking, and legalized abortion, and more. At the time of this writing, a piece of legislation was introduced in Maryland that would decriminalize *death by neglect* up to the first 28 days of a newborn's life, and is without regard to abortion.[6] We are now seeing other states picking up this same kind of wicked legislation. This carries evil laws to a new level. So where does it stop?

Who will stop it?

While we rejoice that America has crossed a threshold with the overturn of Roe v. Wade, the battle continues on the business mountain and at the government gates of the states for the life of the unborn.

The prophet Jeremiah said, *we must winnow at the gates of the land* (Jer. 15:7).

God values people created in His image, and for whom He gave His only begotten Son. As kings and priests, we are mantled to thresh and winnow wickedness. Our godly words and intercession are the spiritual teeth of a threshing instrument.

Satan is *like* a roaring lion looking for whom he can devour (1 Peter 5:8). But Jesus is the Lion of the tribe of Judah who has prevailed over the wicked one. He is standing at the gates as an arrow with His Father to close the gates of demonic intrusion, winnow wickedness, and restore life.

The King of Glory wants to come into our cities. He is looking for His Body to stand with Him in the Father's purposes for individuals, cities, and society.

Will you join Him?

Pray with me: *Father, forgive us for any place where we have neglected our part and role at the gates with You and Your Son. Teach us to step fully into our true identity and Kingdom purpose for the well-being of Your earth. Teach us how to thresh and winnow wickedness that is devouring the life of this generation that is so precious to You. In Jesus' name. Amen.*

To Ponder:

- *What gate is Father calling you to stand at with Him?*
- *Which area of culture do you feel you want to impact most?*
- *In what way is Jesus calling you to increase His influence with individuals, community, or culture?*

5

THE MOUNTAIN OF THE LORD

"The earth will be filled with the knowledge of the glory of God as the waters cover the sea." – Habakkuk 2:14

I n the Spring of 2013, a magazine publication of Christ for the Nations called *The Voice* featured an article by author and speaker Lance Wallnau. The article was titled, *"Get Out of the Church! It's Time to Take Nations!"*[1] The first time I had heard Lance speak was at a small church I attended in Plano, TX, a few years prior. His message was dynamic and clear – the Church must engage a fresh thrust to disciple nations.

Wallnau's message emphasized the Church's need to take back the seven mountains of culture. It was a clarion call being echoed by others, too, like Johnny Enlow. Books such as *The Seven Mountain Prophecy, The Seven Mountain Mandate, Invading the Seven Mountains with Intercession,* and many more fueled a new narrative in Church culture. You could feel a fresh move of the Holy Spirit rolling in.

It was refreshing to hear the message to "get involved!" When I was growing up in the 1960's, the cultural motto was "don't get involved." Unfortunately, rather than the Church standing up to "cultivate and keep" the mountains of influence, that cultural motto seeped into an already growing passivity in the Church regarding cultural issues. This left the gates of Hades wide open to fill the vacuum left by the Church.

The result was seen in ungodly laws being passed, such as the legalization of abortion, the banning of prayer and Bible reading from public schools, Darwinism replacing the teaching of Creationism, and a false separation of Church and state. As the Church kept silent waiting for the rapture, America became a nation inundated with sorcery and perversion.

Many are now waking up and speaking up to take back our culture from the ravaging of evil agendas.

We have lost much ground but with God all things are possible. Through decades of intercession and a recent explosion of believers activated for Kingdom movement, we are now beginning to see a turn of the tide. With the current overturn of Roe v. Wade and other recent victories, such as freedom of public prayer, we have made a breach in the enemy's wall. **It is now time to thrust forward in Kingdom purposes for life and society.**

GOD'S HEART FOR ALL NATIONS IS TO REFLECT THE RADIANCE OF HIS GOODNESS AND GLORY.

God's heart for all nations is to reflect the radiance of His goodness and glory. Each nation carries a unique reflection of Him.

The mountains of culture are meant to be *ministers of God's love and blessing for nurturing that reflection and life in all of society.* The mountains of culture are to help families and communities flourish in well-being and prosperity. But when predator agendas take over, that ceases.

THE CHIEF MOUNTAIN IS GOD'S HOUSE

Scripture teaches that the most prominent mountain over ALL others is the mountain of the Lord. The prophet Isaiah called it the *chief of all mountains*. The Hebrew word for *chief* (*ros*) means: *head, beginning, or principal*. God's Mountain refers to the dwelling place of His glory and His throne. This means that all other mountains are to function under the *headship of God's glory and His throne*.

*"Now it will come about that in the last days, the mountain of the house of the Lord will be established as the **chief of the mountains**, and will be raised above the hills; and all the nations will stream to it. And many peoples will come and say, '**Come, let us go** up to the mountain of the Lord, to the **house** of the God of Jacob; that He may **teach** us concerning His **ways** and that we may walk in His **paths**.' For the **law** will go forth from Zion and the word of the Lord from Jerusalem. And He will **judge** between the nations, and will **render decisions** for many peoples; and they will **hammer** their swords into **plowshares** and their spears into **pruning hooks**. Nation will not lift up sword against nation, and never again will they learn war."* – Isaiah 2:2-4 (emphasis mine)

The Lord's Mountain is the place where He dwells. It is His house ... which means it includes His *household, us!* The word *house* (Heb. *bayit*) means: *temple, household,* **or** *family.* Oh my! Do you now see the significance of our identity and position as God's sons and daughters regarding all the mountains? As His household we are to carry His glory and voice into all the other mountains. Remember what we read in Psalm 72? **God's goal is for the mountains of culture to bring peace to the nations.**

The Father sends His sons and daughters to the mountains to release His peace into society and into people's lives. Peace is not compromise with evil, or a "peace at any cost." Peace is wholeness and completeness. The world is crying for "world peace," but peace can only be found in one place – the *Prince of Peace* whose throne is the dwelling place of God on the mountain of the Lord.

We are ambassadors of peace to the nations as we engage the mountains of culture.

In Isaiah's word, you can even see all the mountains of influence represented:

- **Media** – *"peoples will say, 'Come and let us go...'"*
- **Family** – *"to the house"*
- **Education** – *"He will teach us"*
- **Arts & Entertainment** – *"His ways"*
- **Commerce** – *"His paths"* (routes)
- **Government** – *"law, judge, render decisions"*

Look, too, at what Hebrews 12:22-24 tells us that about our identity as believers:

"But you have come to Mount Zion and to the city of the living God, the heavenly Jerusalem, and to myriads of angels, to the general assembly and church of the firstborn who are enrolled in heaven, and to God, the Judge of all, and to the spirits of the righteous made perfect, and to Jesus, the mediator of a new covenant, and to the sprinkled blood, which speaks better than the blood of Abel."

This is not a future word but a present reality of our position in covenant with God as His household! Our position is connected to His glory, to angelic ministry, to the cloud of witnesses, to His justice, and to the power of Jesus' blood.

I don't think that we, as the Body of Christ, have even begun to discover and walk in all that Father has given us!

Let's look a little more at the details of God's Mountain.

1 – YAHWEH STANDS ABOVE ALL OTHER GODS

God's Mountain is chief because He is Chief. He is the Head, the beginning and the principal One. He is not equal to other gods. He is the Most High and He doesn't share His glory with another. The first three of the LORD's Ten Commandments deal with the worship of Him alone (Ex. 20:2-17):

- *I am the LORD thy God; you shall have **no other gods** before Me.*

- *You shall make no graven images or likenesses* (for idol worship).

- *You shall not take the LORD your God's name in vain* (falsely, as nothing).

"You are worthy, our Lord and God, to receive glory, honor, and power, for You created all things, and for Your pleasure they were created and exist." – Revelation 4:11 (TPT)

The Greek word here for **Lord** (*kyrios*) means: *master, one who has the power of deciding a matter, possessor, owner.* Our Lord, Creator and Father alone is worthy of our worship.

The battle for the seven mountains is a war over who will be worshiped, and which heaven will be accessed by people – God's heaven, or the heavens where the prince of the power of the air dwells.

2 – THE SON ROARS FROM HIS THRONE

God's Mountain (Zion) is where Jesus, the King of Glory, sits at the right hand of the Father on the throne governing all things. Amos 1:2 says that the Lord "roars" from Zion. He roars for righteousness, truth, and justice. He roars against wickedness. His roar is the sound of deliverance. His roar echoes across the land to restore the fear of the Lord.

God's dwelling isn't only in heavenly Zion, however, but in us as His temple on earth. We are spiritually connected to heavenly Zion where we are seated with Christ. If He is roaring, we are roaring too. He is roaring through us.

3 – JESUS' RULE CARRIES THE HEART OF THE FATHER

The *nature* of the Lord's Mountain is a household ... **God is a "family Man."** He is a Father and filters everything through His Fathering care. He does everything through the bond of covenant. He works with, and through, covenant sons and daughters – through a blood covenant cut between the Father and the Son into which we are brought into as family.

As His family, we take His heart into all the realms of earth, motivated by His love.

Since His mountain is the *head* of all mountains, then all other mountains are to operate in the *nature* **of His Fathering care.** They are to help "parent" (nurture) society in righteousness, peace, and joy. These are expressions of His Kingdom. Each mountain has a God-given design for doing this. We will look more at these designs in the chapters ahead.

The cultural mountains today are, unfortunately, reflecting the "parenting" of other gods. "Parenting styles" reflect who is being worshiped.

Other gods are not interested in the well-being of people's lives and nations, but God is.

How government operates, for example, reflects what spiritual beliefs are valued, whether Humanism, Marxism, Christianity, etc. Likewise, what media and education convey reflects their goals and values, too. What do they promote? Is it true and life-giving? Or is it *fake news* and driven with ungodly agendas?

This goes for all the mountains of influence. We must discern whether they are operating with the Spirit of life, or the spirit of error and destruction. We must discern the spiritual "parenting" of that mountain and change what needs to be changed.

Remember, *mountains are dwelling places of the seen and the unseen.* What is being "hosted" reflects in all aspects of its operations and influence. A Scriptural example of this would be Mount Zion called the *city of the Great King* (that being, Jehovah, Ps. 48:2), versus Babylon, known as the *"habitation of devils and hold of every foul spirit* (Rev. 18:2).

Cities have natural and spiritual atmospheres according to their activities. You can sense the spiritual atmosphere of a city, whether as being pleasant and Godly, or as being dark or unsafe.

> FATHER WANTS ALL CITIES AND NATIONS TO EXPERIENCE HIS LOVE.

Father wants all cities and nations to experience the life of His love and nearness.

EQUIPPING FATHER'S HOUSEHOLD IN HIS GLORY

I once heard Kenneth Copeland say that every believer is to be a *faith specialist* – to be expert in faith in whatever they do. To be a specialist of anything requires training.

Our Father wants His household trained for their purpose and calling. For this reason, Jesus has gifted and appointed some to be *apostles, prophets, evangelists, pastors and teachers* for their role to equip the faith specialists (believers) on every mountain of culture. These five gifts are called the *five-fold equipping ministries.*

Their training is not to teach people to stay inside the four walls of the Church, but to *go into all the world and minister God's glory there!*

These five are also gatekeepers on the mountain of the Lord.

God doesn't want us ill-equipped, untrained, and ignorant of our Kingdom identity and purpose. Unfortunately, much of the Church has been just that. As in the Apostle Paul's day, doctrinal error and compromise with worldly philosophies has kept many ignorant of God's truth for their lives. Only in recent years has there been a restored expression of the five-fold ministries, and with it is coming a greater equipping of the saints!

The pastoral gift has borne the care of Church almost solely for generations. I am grateful for every good and faithful pastor but they can't do this immense job alone. Nor did Jesus intend them to do so. Many shepherds have been overwhelmed by the labor and quit. Many sheep have been hurt beneath a one-man structure never intended by the Lord. Some of that hurt has been because those called to be prophets or evangelists were functioning as pastors, but weren't gifted for that position. There is a difference in the function of each.

Jesus gave a five-fold team with the foundation being the apostles and prophets with Jesus as the Cornerstone. He gave teachers, evangelists and pastors to work with the apostles and prophets to help build up the house, rightly fit together as a habitation of God's glory in the earth (Eph. 2:19-20).

These ministry gifts are called by God to be a team that trains God's household to function as an apostolic, prophetic, evangelistic, shepherding, and discipling company on every other mountain. They are mantled to train God's family for the works of service that *God's people* are to do wherever they are in culture. There are even five-fold gifts that operate not only on the mountain of the Lord, but on every other mountain.

Jesus wants His Body strong and well-equipped for life and Kingdom labor. Discipleship and fellowship is a needed part of every believer's life for spiritual growth. Satan has worked to keep believers ignorant, offended and distracted from the works they are to do, but we are entering a new day of equipping for greater works as sons and daughters of glory.

ALL MOUNTAINS HAVE ADVERSARIES

When ancient Israel went in to possess their promised land, they had to remove seven nations greater than themselves: the Hittites, Girgashites, Amorites, Canaanites, Perizzites, Hivites, and the Jebusites (Deut. 7:1; Acts 13:19). Each of these people groups opposed Yahweh and His people. They were described as warlike, wicked, and worshiped demon gods. They filled the land with witchcraft, perversion and child sacrifice in worship to Baal, Asherah, Molech, as well as many other gods (Deut. 12:2-3, 30-31; 18:9-12).

Nevertheless, God's people conquered those enemies! How? Through God's power and presence that they hosted as they carried the ark of His glory, listening to His strategies for possessing the land, city by city.

We must see God as greater than the enemy. As we saw earlier, that worship pattern was a foreshadow of the cross. If we want victory for our lives and nations it will take us picking up our own cross and following Christ into culture (Matt. 16:24).

> **WE MUST SEE GOD AS GREATER THAN THE ENEMY!**

We triumph by listening to His voice and carrying His glory.

Israel, who had been delivered from bondage in Egypt, became the *agents of deliverance* for Canaan. So too, we who have been delivered from bondage in sin and death now become *God's agents of deliverance* for the world around us. This is not by our might or power, but as willing vessels of God's love in whom His Spirit dwells.

Those ancient Canaanite tribes no longer exist today, but the principalities that ruled them do. They, along with a host of other demonic forces, continue to infiltrate nations and social structures around the world, seeking human cooperation to give them legal right of access.

Much of the Church for a long time has not wanted to talk about evil entities, but they are realities that must be dealt with. After all, Jesus already defeated them at the cross. We are only enforcing His triumph over them through prayer and righteous action. At no other time in history has there been such an overt and concerted assault on humanity by evil.

Every arena of culture has demonic opposition to God's ways and presence. That opposition can be discerned by what people are experiencing. Is our community experiencing freedom or oppression? Love or violence? Are people flourishing or is their prosperity and safety declining?

We have been given authority over the enemy to bring God's goodness to nations. We are here to make a difference as to what kind of influence comes into our homes and society.

THE WAR AGAINST THE HOUSE OF GOD

There is a war against faith in the one true God. We see it in every area of American culture today. As mentioned, one of ancient Israel's enemies was the *Amorite*. The Amorites worshiped *Baal*, which means: *lord, master, husband*. Baal was Yahweh's arch enemy in Canaan who continually tried to divorce the heart of Israel from the LORD. The strategy of this principality was to try and win Israel's trust for blessing and provision through him instead of from Yahweh.

This ancient spiritual enemy seeks the high place of faith with the intent of *divorcing* people's hearts from the love of God. It works to seduce people's minds to trust another *way* as truth and provision for happiness. Psalm 16:25 says, *"There is a way that seems right to man but the end of it is death."*

Some teach the *mountain of faith* as including all religions, including Christianity. I have chosen, however, to separate the Mountain of the Lord from other religions. God doesn't share His dwelling place with other gods. All roads do not lead to Yahweh. He has many names, but none of them is Allah, or Buddha, or Krishna.

What is similar to all faiths, however, is their impact on culture. The spiritual beliefs of any society will influence every other part of its culture – from the laws that are legislated, to the family structure, to its social and educational values, to its arts and entertainment.

> THE SPIRITUAL BELIEFS OF ANY SOCIETY WILL INFLUENCE EVERY OTHER PART OF ITS CULTURE.

In ancient civilizations, cities were built around the temple of the gods they worshipped, which directly influenced all of society.

This means that whoever stands as *lord* in realms of faith gets the rest of culture. In India we see how Hinduism influences key aspects of culture such as the social caste system, family dynamics, and festivities. In Muslim nations we see how society functions under Shariah law. So too, early American life was shaped by God's Word, including its government structure, family values, and foundations of education.

Where did the nations get this model of faith and culture? God! In heaven everything is centered around God's throne and His Temple. It fills all of heaven and its activities with God's glory. Heaven's glory pattern is the structure for earth. When Israel journeyed through the wilderness, all the tribes camped around the Tabernacle where God's glory dwelled with them. God was their center of everything.

Satan uses that same pattern with world religions under his dominion. Nations under his lordship reflect the expression of his oppression against life, freedom and prosperity. People and nations whose God is the Lord, however, have life and blessing.

Psalm 33:12 says, *"Blessed is the nation whose God is the LORD..."* **If we want to see America restored, we must restore faith in God.** America needs Father's house to show up in the public square. The voice of faith specialists must rise for the sake of our regions and national family.

To stand with Father at the gates of the faith mountain means being witnesses of His love in Christ. It means sharing the good news and truth that Jesus is the (only) Way to the Father, and that He is the true Lord of heaven and earth.

"There is one Lord, one faith, one baptism, one God and Father of all who is over all and through all and in all." – Eph. 4:5-6

Father wants us to know His ways. *Jesus is His Way* and Jesus Himself, along with Holy Spirit will teach us the ways of the Father. God wants us to share His love with the world around us. He wants to bring many sons and daughters to glory. As Father's household we are to declare His goodness, heal the sick, raise the dead, cleanse the leper. We are to heal the brokenhearted and minister freedom to those trapped in the death snares of Satan and his dark hosts.

We are in a sending time. We must go with the Word of the Lord in our mouth to bring God's peace to every house and every nation.

Here are some keys for standing at the gates of this mountain:

- Love the Lord with all your heart, soul, mind, and strength, and others as yourself (Matt. 12:30-31).

- Put on the mind of Christ and the whole armor of God (Eph. 6).

- Discern worldly ideologies and doctrines of demons that shut out the Holy Spirit. Such doctrines include Cessationism, Replacement Theology, hyper-grace, New Age spirituality, and "all roads lead to God"… to name a few.

- Stand for oneness in Christ; refute elitism, isolation, and selfish ambition.

- Discern witchcraft operating in the Church through manipulation, control, and people pleasing.

- Ask Holy Spirit to align you with Godly five-fold ministries: apostles, prophets, evangelists, pastors, and Godly teachers.

- Help disciple people in faith, truth, love, and the power of the Holy Spirit.

- Evangelize; seek God for fresh strategies for reaching cities and regions.

- Heal the sick, cleanse lepers, raise the dead, cast out demons.

FINDING YOUR PLACE ON
THE MOUNTAINS OF CULTURE

In the following chapters, we are going to take a brief look at the other mountains of influence and Father's heart for each one. It is by no means an in-depth study but is meant to awaken our hearts to His true and beautiful designs for all of society.

To know His heart is to reveal His glory. **Every mountain of culture is meant to reveal God's Fathering care and His glory so that nations function in their true, God-given design.**

You have a God-given design and so does your family, city, and nation. This means they need agents of love, healing and deliverance who will minister God's peace to them.

You and I are mantled and called to touch individuals, communities, and society in some way. If you are not sure what area the Lord wants to touch through your voice and gifts, ask the Holy Spirit to show you. He may quicken something to you as we look at the other mountains of culture. I pray He does.

Pray with me: *Father, teach me to worship You in spirit and in truth. Teach me to love You with all my heart, soul, mind, and strength. Teach me to love the world around me and be a bold minister of Your heart, ways, truth and love to them. In Jesus' name. Amen.*

To Ponder:

- *Do you believe that Jesus is the only way to the Father?*
- *What is the Holy Spirit speaking to you about His call on your life for this season?*
- *Do you struggle in trusting God? If so, why?*

6

THE FATHER'S DESIGN FOR GOVERNMENT

*"For by Him all things were created, both in the heavens and on earth,
visible and invisible, whether thrones, or dominions, or rulers,
or authorities—all things have been created
through Him and for Him." – Colossians 1:16*

We can only serve the Father's purposes when we know His heart. Our Father has a glorious design for all things to function and flourish with life, including government. Of all places in culture, government should manifest God's heart and glory since **His glory and government are embodied together in the King** who sits on the throne of heaven and earth.

As we read in Colossians 1:16, all authorities both in heaven and on earth were created *by* the Son and *for* the Son upon whose shoulders all government rests (Isaiah 9:6). Authorities are not given authority to do their own pleasure or purpose. They are given to do the will of Christ.

> **ALL AUTHORITIES IN HEAVEN AND EARTH WERE CREATED BY THE SON AND FOR THE SON.**

Scripture teaches us that all authority is given by *God* as *delegated* (assigned) authority. The Hebrew word for **God** (*El*) means: **first authority**. God is the First Authority in everything, whether it is the government of our personal life, our family, church, business, or civil leaders (Rom. 13:1). Delegated authority is one that is assigned and accountable to the highest authority – God.

Every authority on earth is created for the purpose of protecting and prospering life. All governments and authorities have a God given purpose to minister His life-giving values to everything under their jurisdiction. Jesus' own rule is described as being wonderful, full of counsel and strength, as carrying the Father's heart, and ministering peace. Jesus carries Abba's purposes into all that He does to ensure the wholeness of all that is under His governance, which is everything.

This is the standard He sets for *all* who are in authority.

SERVANT LEADERSHIP

Godly government is meant to spring from a heart of love and serving. Jesus demonstrated this Himself who came as a Servant Leader. Please understand that love is not compromise, entitlement, or enablement. Love is patient and kind, but protects boundaries and stands strong against what destroys life. Godly love is not namby-pamby.

Governing is a solemn charge to ensure the safety and well-being of the local, state, and national family. Authorities who govern in a way that reveres the Highest Authority are a blessing to the people. Authorities who oppose God's values for life bring a curse upon the land. They cause life and prosperity to wither.

Right now, I get daily e-mails warning me about *"the world's greatest crisis ever seen with food shortages."* Worldwide food shortages, supply chain problems, hyperinflation, and oil crisis are just a few of the problems facing many nations – problems that are often preventable when good government is at the helm.

> EVERY AUTHORITY ON EARTH IS CREATED FOR THE PURPOSE OF PROTECTING AND PROSPERING LIFE.

Sometimes a crisis is made by natural circumstances beyond anyone's control. Sometimes a crisis is made by devastating government policies, such as seen in Venezuela under Hugo Chavez. By 2019, ninety percent of Venezuelans were living below the poverty line because of his policies.

We are here to prosper life, not destroy it.

This should be your litmus test for who you vote for – do they prosper or plunder the well-being of society? Whose pocket are they lining? Do they revere God, or another god?

While Scripture says we are to submit to the governing authorities that God has established, it also says that *His* authorities *"hold no terror for those who do right, but for those who do wrong" (Rom. 13:3).* We must recognize that there are those in office that God Himself did not establish. If authorities do not support what is right in His sight, then they are in rebellion against the First Authority. This is why Peter and the other apostles said, *"We ought to obey God rather than man"* (Acts 5:29).

While we are to always honor and respect people, if authorities oppose the ways of God, the Highest Authority, then we are not to comply with their rebellion. This applies to civil, corporate, and family authority. That may sound harsh but think of those who submitted in silence to Hitler or Joseph Stalin. Those who didn't submit were heroes who hid Jews and helped people escape. They moved for freedom not just for themselves but for the world around them until freedom was gained and wickedness was winnowed.

We must be vigilant regarding ungodliness in authority that leads to tyranny. This includes not accepting abuse in the home against women and children.

THE KNOWLEDGE AND REVERENCE OF GOD

King Solomon said, *"The fear of the Lord is the beginning of wisdom, and the knowledge of the Holy One is understanding"* (Pro. 9:10). The word **knowledge** (Heb. *da'at*) is not just knowing about something, but is an intimate knowledge of God through relationship and fellowship with Him. It conveys the idea of covenant. No doubt, Solomon learned that from his father, King David, who governed a nation with a heart that revered covenant with Yahweh.

David described the fear of the LORD as being **clean** (Ps. 19:9). **Clean means: *what is pure, without mixture or evil, without compromise or selfish ambition.*** The Hebrew word for *unclean* (*tame*) means: *what is defiled, polluted and what strongly surrounds with chaos.* The chaos in culture we see today is because of an unclean spirit released on the land. And as they say – it all starts with leadership.

King David didn't want a reign of chaos but of divine blessing. He knew that the reverence of the First Authority opens the treasure house of victory, wisdom, strength and stability (Isa. 33:6). These are needed for governing.

King Solomon wrote, *"The fear of the LORD is to hate evil; pride, arrogance, the evil way, and the perverted mouth I hate"* (Pro. 8:13). Government can either be a beloved King David or an evil Nero.

Psalm 14:34 says, *"Righteousness exalts a nation, but sin is a reproach to any people."* And Proverbs 29:2 says, *"When the righteous are in authority, the people rejoice; but when the wicked rule, the people groan."*

Revering God means doing what is right through a sense of respect for God. It springs from an internal awareness of a personal responsibility of being in relationship with Him. To love and worship God is to revere Him. More than

> WE MUST BE VIGILANT REGARDING UNGODLINESS IN AUTHORITY.

once in my life I have been stopped by the fear of the Lord from taking a wrong action or saying a wrong word. At other times that fear was a holy compelling to do something!

When the Church begins to operate more in the fear of the LORD there will be a lot more righteous action going on in culture!

GLORIFYING GOD'S NAME

In Revelation 15:5-6, the Apostle John's experience in heaven included seeing those who had overcome the anti-Christ system (the beast). He wrote, *"And they sing the song of Moses, the servant of God, and the song of the Lamb saying: 'Great and marvelous are your works, O Lord God, the Almighty. Just and true are your ways, O King of the nations. Who shall not fear You, O Lord, and glorify Your name? For You alone are holy. For all nations shall come and worship before You, for Your judgments have been manifested.'"*

As we near the return of Christ, we will see His righteous judgments manifesting more in the earth, and we will know they are right. God's Word says that through them the nations learn righteousness (Isa. 26:9). We will see greater boldness in God's people for His name's sake, and we will also know what it is to overcome as we love not our lives even unto death (Rev. 12:11).

What an amazing experience John had in hearing the triumphant song of Moses and the Lamb filling heaven's throne room. Moses was one of Israel's greatest civil leaders. He was also God's agent of deliverance for a nation. We need more leaders who are God's agents of deliverance! That, however, requires humility and the reverence of God.

Moses was said to be more humble than any other man (Num. 12:3). Moses understood his governing role as a *servant leader* under Yahweh's authority and was accountable to Him for everything. He operated by the fear of the Lord and so led God's people out of bondage. As he followed God's leadership, his nation experienced miracle after miracle. Did he make mistakes? Yes. But his heart's cry was, *"Show me Your glory!"* (Ex. 33:18)

To see God's glory is to see His heart, nature, and ways. Looking at His glory is life transforming. Transformed people transform culture.

WHEN AUTHORITIES SERVE THEMSELVES, IT LEADS TO EVERY KIND OF ABUSE, FRAUD, AND OPPRESSION.

In today's world, it's hard to imagine what the world would be like if all leaders operated in the knowledge and reverence of God. But this is what Father intends for the sake of the people. God values people. He hears their cries for help and justice. He hears the cry from the blood of the innocent, the martyred, and the unborn.

He hears the cries of the trafficked and abused children. He feels the pain of broken hearts and broken dreams. He sees the plight of the innocent … *and* the ways of the guilty.

When authorities serve themselves, it leads to every kind of abuse, fraud, and oppression. We've seen this operating in unprecedented levels in the past few years like a runaway train – from infanticide to election fraud to medical tyranny, and much more. It's time to stop that train and bring in the train of God's glory!

James 3:16 says, *wherever there is selfish ambition you will find every kind of evil.* We must pray for all in authority – whether civil, corporate, familial, or in the Church – that they might have a God encounter and *fear of the Lord* for the well-being of everyone!

Governing authorities will be held accountable for what they have done with the authority given them. Those who have opened the gates of hell through wicked legislation and actions will be held responsible. We must pray for their turn to righteousness, as well as for justice.

GOVERNMENT GATEKEEPERS

The gatekeepers on this mountain include: local, state, and federal authorities such as city council members, mayors, county clerks, commissioners, sheriffs, precinct chairs, and state representatives. It includes senators, governors, attorney generals, judges (district, appellate, circuit, magistrate, and supreme courts), law enforcement, and the military. It also includes many other offices that work in tandem with these.

However, these are not the only gatekeepers! Here in the United States, we are a Republic. As believers, we have dual calling as citizens of heaven and citizens of our nation to be gatekeepers. We are to be watchmen who govern spiritually and naturally through intercession and action regarding policies and legislation.

We govern through voting and civic action. We elect our officials to do what is right in representing us. If they act corruptly then we must speak up, loudly, and remove them if necessary.

It is *our* responsibility to elect good officials *and* hold them responsible to follow through in caring for the people. If we do nothing, or if we turn a blind eye to corruption, then we share responsibility for what happens.

It is proven that if the righteous do not show up, evil will reign. If the light doesn't shine, then darkness prevails. It's not rocket science. **The Church must show up in all areas of society, including government.**

We must vote in local, state, and national elections. What we do, or neglect to do, has a direct impact on the destiny of our families, cities, and nation. We determine our future and that of our children, grandchildren, and great grandchildren. We must think legacy because Father does.

> WE MUST VOTE IN LOCAL, STATE, AND NATIONAL ELECTIONS.

In the recent state primary elections of my own congressional district, it was estimated that less than 20% of registered voters voted. Worse yet, only 8% turned out to vote in my county's 2022 local elections! And I am in a major conservative county in the Dallas, TX metroplex!

This is a huge part of why America is in the state that it's in – people are not involved. **Father's Household MUST show up for issues involving laws and legislation, and vote His values!**

Many people don't vote because they don't think it makes a difference, or they don't care, or they don't like any of the candidates. But God told Israel to care for the prosperity of the land where He put them, and they, too, would prosper. Even when they were in Babylon!

Some feel politics is not a Christian's concern, but **all political issues are first biblical issues.** Borders are biblical issues. Abortion is a biblical issue. Gender is a biblical issue, as are family, education, and business practices.

Knowing and speaking what Father says about these issues is part of our standing with Him at the gate of this mountain to close the portals of hell and open the gates of glory.

TIME TO RIDE WITH JESUS!

Jesus is not indifferent to the plight of nations. Scripture says He rides in His majesty to *defend truth, humility, and justice (Ps. 45:4)*. After all, He IS the government of God! As the Last Adam, He is on the move to carry out the Genesis charge to prosper and protect seed. We are to move with Him.

Jesus' value system for rulers is to be, *"I'm here to help you succeed with a future and a hope."* It is not, *"How can you benefit me?"* This is why revering God is needed on this mountain as it protects the heart from corruption and self-serving comprise.

God has a lot to say about the way government should run! From Genesis to Revelation, the Bible is about governments, kings, and kingdoms and how they respond to God and govern nations. Again, some say the Church shouldn't be involved in politics. But the truth is we are mantled to do something! I hope you've seen by now that you and I have a personal, spiritual, *and* social responsibility.

When the wicked sit in seats of government, they make ruling decisions that devour life. When the godly sit in seats of government, they are able to draw strategies and blueprints from heaven to make ruling decisions that are just, true, and empower lives.

Who would you rather have sitting at the helm of your city, state, and nation?

When laws become harmful to the people, when government suppresses more than it empowers, and when mandates defy common sense and deny citizens their true rights, you know that government has become a predator rather than a protector. Again, it is not rocket science.

People across America and around the world are beginning to stand up against governments that operate in evil to prosper themselves rather than prosper the people. Many are rising to bring needed accountability and justice. The Spirit of the Son is moving for justice – we must move with Him for the sake of the earth that we are charged to prosper.

PREDATOR ON THE MOUNTAIN

One of the predators that seeks roles of government is the nature of the Hittite – an enemy of ancient Israel. The name *Hittite* means: *terror, fear*. This is not the same as the healthy fear of the Lord. Rather, it is a terror invoked by domination and control.

This spiritual adversary works through authorities driven by a spirit of greed and its lust for power, glory, and money. It manifests as governing overreach and tyranny. Scripture says that greed brings grief to the whole family, including the family of a nation (Pro. 15:27). Greed is a ruling spirit that operates through lies, fraud, dishonesty, *murder*, and oppression for its own gain (Jer. 22:17).

> CORRUPTION IN GOVERNMENT IS NOT JUST ABOUT HUMAN DECISIONS, BUT A SPIRITUAL ALIGNMENT.

Habakkuk 2:5 describes those ruling with lust for wealth as *self-indulgent and arrogant, whose words are like death, and never satisfied with what they take.* They gather up nations and swallow the people through deceit.

Some also refer to this as a *"jezebel spirit"* – referring to an Old Testament queen of Israel who operated in greed and advanced evil agendas for personal gain. It refers to an ungodly spiritual alignment that can operate through both men and women in positions of authority. Jezebel was a worshiper of Baal.

Today, this spirit has invaded not just our government, but corporations, media, and public education. It has invaded every aspect of culture.

Father says we are to guard against greed, corruption and unjust practices that bring terror and fear to the land. It is a spiritual oppressor using fear to get its way, and fear is a spirit. That fear can be fear for your life, financial fears, health fears, fear for your future well-being, and more.

Corruption in government is not just about human decisions but a spiritual alignment. Remember, all mountains operate through the god (or God) that is worshiped, and who is "fathering" them. Human decisions are linked with spiritual alignments. Ungodly laws, greed and tyranny reflect ungodly spiritual alignments.

Governing systems, such as Marxism, is aligned with a demon principality. Its very symbol is the **sickle and hammer**. A sickle is a *harvest* tool. The heavy hammer of Marxist laws is joined to the sickle for harvesting the wealth of nations, wealth that lines the coffers of wicked leaders while impoverishing the people.

The very tenets of Marxism exalt government as a nation's god. It purports itself as the "rightful" parent and educator of the nation's children. It establishes government as the owner of a nation's land, economy, business and medical availability. It defrauds in order to swallow the people.

History proves the tens of millions that have been slain, and the destruction of social well-being in nations dominated by this political demon – from Russia to Cuba to Venezuela to China. It's also hammering its way through American culture with a harvest in site.

Will it succeed?

It will if no one stops it.

We each have a part in this spiritual war for our nation, and the nations.

Some sitting in government want to speak out but are afraid. We must pray for them and give them courage by our own supportive words.

CONTENDING FOR RIGHT VERDICTS AT THE GATES

"Righteousness and justice are the foundation of Your throne; lovingkindness and truth go before Your face. Blessed are the people who hear the joyful sound! They walk in the light of Your countenance." – Psalm 89:14-15

Father is looking for those willing to help contend for right verdicts at the gates where ruling decisions are made. As the Body of the One who is just, we are all called to put our hand to the labor of justice in some way.

Here are some things needed as we stand at this gate with Jesus:

- Decree this mountain to be set free into God's original design for it.
- Pray for revival and reformation in government. Pray for repentance and the fear of the Lord on every person in congress, senate, judicial seats, and every other place and role in governing – from local to state to federal seats.
- Pray for those in authority to make wise, selfless decisions and to love the people they govern. Pray for salvation and the fear of the Lord in their lives and decisions.

- Vote and support those who hold to biblical values in local, state, and federal elections.

- Attend city council meetings; write or call your representatives and senators on current issues.

- Be a precinct chair person, or run for office!

- Support godly leaders through elections; join a righteous movement.

- Pray for the outpouring of God's glory!

God wants to bless the nations! In this end-time harvest, God is raising up a company of sons and daughters filled with the Spirit of the Son who will govern with the Father's heart and ways. He is lifting up a standard of wisdom through them. This company will be both loving and bold for truth, especially for the sake of the children.

Pray with me: *Father, winnow out wickedness from my own heart, and from those sitting in seats of government. Send Your fire to activate me into action for my community, state, and nation through governing involvement! Turn the hearts of those in roles of authority to reflect Your goodness. Send angels to help us battle for our regions that belong to You so that Your glory dwells in this land. In Jesus' name. Amen.*

To Ponder:

- *How involved are you in voting for the decisions impacting your region?*

- *How often do you pray for those in authority?*

- *How much does the reverence of Father guide your decisions?*

7

THE FATHER'S HEART FOR EDUCATION

"Take hold of instruction; do not let go.
Guard her, for she is your life."
Proverbs 4:13

C hanging times creates changes in activities. Because of the threat of recent global food shortages, my husband and I decided to start our own garden in our tiny backyard. For me, even plastic plants are a challenge to keep "fresh" let alone grow something real. My husband, however, determined to succeed in our endeavor, and so set himself to research how to grow vegetables.

I was amazed at the entire system he put together for our plants to succeed – from the method of using "grow bags" to the proper mix of soil to creating an elaborate drip watering system for nurturing specific seeds that would grow in our Texas summer.

Education is much like that. It is an amazing system of applied knowledges for developing the heart and mind of a child for a fruitful destiny. **Education is like food and water for growing the *whole person* so that a child's potential emerges with the greatest development possible.**

God puts a great importance on our development as His children. He wants us to succeed in a life that is fruitful in every way. Education helps nurture that growth. The human heart and mind are incredible things but need words of wisdom, knowledge, and truth for a life to grow to full potential.

As they say, knowledge is power and ignorance leads to poverty. There is a glory of God released in our lives through right education, helping us to grow in *wisdom to full stature*. That education may or may not be formal, but it should support wisdom and truth for developing the whole person in every way.

Righteous teachers and instructors are a gift of God to every generation. Under the guidance of wise teachers, people and nations thrive. Ungodly instruction, however, destroys people and nations.

This is the battle we are fighting in American public schools today.

EDUCATION IS MEANT TO REVEAL GOD

True instruction reveals God in *everything*. It unlocks the treasures of truth hidden in *all* studies and disciplines, both natural and spiritual. The word **truth** (Heb. *emet*) means: the **mother of covenant**. In other words, **true education** is meant to nurture our bond with God. If instruction leads us away from God, then it misses the mark of its purpose, which is to lead us to Him. True education makes us fruitful in our thinking.

For example, reading empowers the ability to discover God's heart through reading His Word. Learning history opens a child's mind to wisdom about the past, present, and even future, and seeing God as the Divine Planner over the generations (Jer. 9:24). In mathematics a child sees God as the brilliant builder of the universe and how those same principles apply to his or her own life. In physics God is known as the Source of all matter and energy and how energy is accessed. In science we see His invisible attributes in what He created (Rom. 1:20). In astronomy we see the testimony of redemption declared night unto night (Ps. 19).

All true knowledge points us to God!

Education in truth in every realm of study empowers a child's life and God-given purpose in this world. All roads don't lead to God, but all education should. Unless we build our children on the foundation of truth then all the education of the world will be as sinking sand to their lives. Some of the world's most educated men are fools headed to hell.

AMERICA'S EARLY EDUCATION

America's founding fathers understood that education founded on God's wisdom is the key to a hopeful future. America was founded on God's Word in every part of society from government to business to family.

Our early forefathers understood that for a free nation to succeed it required an educated and wise people. It's why Benjamin Franklin, when asked what kind of government had just been newly formed here, replied, "A republic, madam, if you can keep it."

> AN IGNORANT PEOPLE WILL CONSENT TO ANYTHING.

This new nation would need an educated and wise people to succeed as a *free* Republic. At the founding of the United States our education system stressed the seven liberal arts of: grammar, logic, and rhetoric, as well as arithmetic, geometry, astronomy, and music as a proper education. Notice that there was no discussion of trying to figure out one's gender identity.

Thomas Jefferson believed only educated citizens could make the American experiment in self-government succeed. Though John Adams believed that education should be of "every rank and class of people down to the lowest and the poorest," and felt it should be a "public care,"[1] it was never thought that it should be taken from the hands of the parents![2]

Listen to more thoughts from our founding fathers on this matter:

- "All I am I owe to my mother. I attribute all my success in life to the moral, intellectual and physical education I received from her." – George Washington

- "A Bible and a newspaper in every house, a good school in every district – all studied and appreciated as they merit are the principal support of *virtue, morality, and civil liberty*." – Benjamin Franklin

While Thomas Jefferson argued that "government derives their just powers from the consent of the governed," he also understood that education is what makes that consent possible.[3]

An ignorant people will consent to anything. Hence, the foolishness at work in our nation's education today is leading this generation down a path of ignorance and stupidity as a people easily controlled by its own consent to evil.

Centuries prior to the founding of our nation, the great reformer, Martin Luther, said this about education, *"I am much afraid that the universities will prove to be the great gates of hell, unless they diligently labor in explaining the Holy Scriptures, and engraving them in the hearts of youth."*[4]

America has experienced tremendous blessing because of the early founding of God's Word in government and education. We have lost ground, however, as our universities have indeed become the gates of hell. We have lost hold of wise instruction. It's time to close these gates of hell and repair the foundation of education by teaching our children God's ways (see Psalm 78).

For our children and our nation to succeed as a free and prosperous people our education must be founded in God's truth. Ignorance is the path to slavery and corruption the road to tyranny.

> WE MUST REPAIR THE FOUNDATION OF EDUCATION BY TEACHING OUR CHILDREN GOD'S WAYS.

Did you know that the first book published in America (1640) was a book titled *The Bay of Psalm Book*? It was a book of Psalms put to rhythm for the purpose of singing Scripture. The early settlers understood the great need for life instruction to begin with worship! It's why our first university in America was a seminary – Harvard, founded in 1636.

The founding colonists and leaders understood that truth was as important to building a society as the wood for building a house. They got that from the Bible!

In the Old Testament, Moses was *commanded* to choose *men of truth* who revered God to hold positions of leadership (Ex. 18:21). The gatekeepers of their cities were righteous rulers and judges (Deut. 16:18).

We are raising the next generation of gatekeepers who will need truth in education to prepare them for their role in culture.

TRAINING OUR CHILDREN

Scripture teaches us that it is the role of parents who are in charge of their child's training (Deut. 6:7). This does not mean that parents themselves have to teach all the scholastic skills, but they are responsible to make sure a *good* and *godly* education is provided.

Our children's instruction is our right and charge as parents. The Bible supports parental rights, not government rights, regarding children. Children belong to God before they belong to us – we are stewards of God's purposes for them. Remember, He is the Author and Finisher of the generations of humanity.

Proverbs 22:6 says, *"Train up a child in the way he should go and when he is old he will not depart from it"* (NKJV).

Training is the parent's responsibility (not the government's) to shape the growth and potential of their seed and lineage.

To *train* a child in the *way he or she should go* involves disciplines in knowledge, skills, manner, and moral character. It includes spiritual understanding and maturity, too. Training should bring children into the true knowledge of God and their identity and purpose in Him.

The word **way** (Heb. *derek*) means: **the door of highest vision**. Education should give a child **vision** for their divine purpose so they can fulfill their calling from God.

One of the Hebrew words for **teach** is *zahar*, which means: *to send out light, to enlighten, including for admonishment and warning*. Light empowers vision for what is the right way to go. This means that a child's training should shine the light on their specific gifts, God-given passions and dreams, unique abilities, and potentials ... **and their character!**

A child's abilities are given to release God's glory through their life work and Kingdom purpose. Right character empowers the success of their gifts.

In the Old Testament when God gave Moses the Tabernacle blueprints, he didn't pick just anyone to build this divine plan on earth. He chose *skilled workers with the spirit of wisdom*.

Wisdom unlocks the glory DNA within our gifts as we partner together with God for His plans. This applies to us and our children. They should be taught this from their earliest years.

People shouldn't wait until they are twenty, thirty, or sixty years old to know how to partner with God in their skills. As we hone our gifts and develop intimacy with God, we are able to build according to God's blueprints for our lives.

There is a glory pattern and DNA within our God-given gifts. They are meant to function with God's glory. We must change the way we think about education and bring God's glory into our training.

There is glory in a child's gifts. This is true for every person, no matter how old. We teach children how to access knowledge through books and the internet, but do they know how to access divine understanding from God's presence for their gifts? They need both. Are they being trained to access divine pictures, sounds, and ideas?

> GIFTS ARE MEANT TO FUNCTION WITH GOD'S GLORY.

In God's presence are blueprints and designs for the works they are to do. This should be the norm for all children, especially a child of God, no matter the age. This should be part of a standard Christian education for all ages!

WATERING ROYAL SEED AND LAUNCHING ROYAL ARROWS

Remember, Father isn't just raising sons and daughters, but a ruling company of covenant sons and daughters. Our children need to be trained in this understanding as part of their academia. Another Hebrew word for *teach* is *yara* which means: *to shoot like an arrow, to direct and instruct, to throw water, to rain.* Remember, children are like arrows in a father's quiver. *Yara* reflects another aspect of how teaching empowers both the "growing" (making) of an arrow and the direction of an arrow's flight path so that it hits a target.

Targets are purposes, goals, and assignments. God's purposes include everything from corporate projects, to medical and scientific discoveries, to art, to engineering, and much more. Without the necessary skills gained through training, divine purpose will be left undone.

A good education is to be linked to a child's calling. This means that education should also be "custom fit" in watering the seed of a child's unique abilities for reaching their fullest potential.

Such an education aids a child to grow to full maturity as it unlocks the potential within them so they can step fully into the significant role God has for them.

We, and our children, are royal seed and arrows to be launched from the quiver of our Father. Unfortunately, government today is using public education to shape children as arrows for demonic agendas.

America's public education system is different than it was when I was a child. In fact, the U.S. Department of Education wasn't even formed until 1979. Public education is now a *system* of Humanism driven by Marxist ideology and Darwin's theory of evolution – systems engulfed in *self*-exaltation.

How can children grow into their divine purpose swimming in the waters from Hades, where perversion and narcissism is taught behind closed doors in the classroom? Where children learn that the *school* is the parental truth to whom they are accountable.

Parents are stewards of a seed that belongs to God (Ezek. 18:4). God's enemies want to twist the mind of that seed with ungodly ideas so they do not reach their full potential in bringing forth the works of God into the earth.

Children need confidence. They need vision. A right education gives them that. It gives wings to their dreams and a wind to the sail of their destiny. It not only sets their individual trajectory in life, but a society's education sets the trajectory of society as a whole.

> A RIGHT EDUCATION GIVES WINGS TO DREAMS AND IS WIND TO THE SAIL OF DESTINY.

Education sets the course of a nation, causing it to rise and fall by the leaders that are chosen and choices that are made through either wisdom or ignorance.

We must guard carefully this mountain that sets the trajectory of lives and nations.

DESTINY SPECIALISTS

I call those who labor on this mountain *destiny specialists*. They help people develop the skills for the destiny and Kingdom work they are called to do. Gatekeepers include parents, teachers, coaches, and educational administrators and others who work in the educational field.

Proverbs 18:16 says that a person's gift makes room for him and brings him before great men. As a child matures, there are people that he or she are meant to meet and connect with for divine purposes. Education helps position them and prepares them for that encounter. This is true for us, too, no matter our age.

Even if we missed the opportunity to be educated properly or fully, it is never too late! In fact, our education should never stop. I went back to finish my degrees when I was in my forties and fifties in order to do what I am doing today. I continue to take courses all the time.

I know a woman who recently picked up painting after having left it for many years. She is now creating phenomenal biblical artwork. Her work is inspiring and is known well beyond the walls of her home…and she is eighty years old!

American author and educator John Taylor Gatto once said, **"Nobody gives you an education. If you want one, you have to take it!"**

God is able to restore the years that have been eaten away by the enemy. So too, we must have a mindset for learning and ever-increasing prosperity in spirit, mind, and body.

THE PERIZZITE PREDATOR

Satan has a system of life development for children, too. It's called *false enlightenment*. Another enemy ancient Israel had to defeat was the Perizzites. *Perizzite* means: *unwalled country dweller, open region.*[5] It speaks of having no boundaries, of being "open minded" to *any* thought, philosophy or ideology.

It is the opposite of a dedicated training in the way God intends for a godly and purposeful destiny.

Paul told the Ephesians that we should *"no longer be children, tossed to and fro and carried about with every wind of doctrine, by the trickery of men, in the cunning craftiness of deceitful plotting"* (Eph. 4:14).

Satan works through ungodly philosophies to create *"sons of Belial"* whose minds are guided by darkness. Humanism (man-centeredness) and Darwinism are two such ideologies. *Belial* means: *worthless and foolish* (1 Sam. 2:12). Today we see it manifesting through perverse indoctrinations touted as education while creating a foolish, and even demonized, generation. It is rendering young lives ill-equipped for divine purpose. We must contend for the children's hearts and minds.

Due to COVID mandates in 2020 to 2021, school closings allowed the eyes of parents to see the perverse curriculum being taught in public schools everywhere. Ideologies such as Marxism, Critical Race Theory, the 1619 Project, and Gender Bending Identity are among the few. It includes sexually explicit curriculum, eastern meditation, and sorcery. Instructions from hell are being used to shape children's hearts and minds all the way down to kindergarten. Boys are taught they can be girls and vice versa, and all this being hidden from the parents by the school system.

These are **ideological predators** working to devour the seed of a nation, both intellectually, spiritually, and in moral character. They now openly say they are grooming our children for their agendas. They have been subverting true education and exchanging *how to think* with *what to think* as defined by a *Belial* system of thought.

My six-year-old granddaughter recently shared with me that her public-school teacher instructed them to "imagine using their Harry Potter wand." The Harry Potter series may seem captivating with creativity, but it is indoctrination into witchcraft. It opens children to demonic torment and activity in their lives, and leads to spiritual bondage.

We must realize how much Satan is after the children. When this generation rises in truth it will be a great threat to his kingdom, and he knows it.

The demonic world is real, though most of the Church has not wanted to talk about it. But now we must talk about it. Deal with it – for the sake of the children who are being carried away by every wind of doctrine of demons. The American education system is creating a Babylonian nation and "the habitation of every foul spirit." This is not America's destiny, nor the destiny of our children.

Our nation is in a spiritual war for the minds and hearts of our children. It's time to pray and take action. It's time to close the gates of Hades and winnow wickedness from the mountain of education.

A people who are morally, intellectually, and spiritually corrupt raise leaders of their own image. This destroys a nation.

Albert Einstein said, **"Most people say that it is the intellect which makes a great scientist. They are wrong: it is character."**

Proverbs 28:2 says, *"When there is moral rot within a nation, its government topples easily. But wise and knowledgeable leaders bring stability."*

Corrupt morals and philosophies taught on the mountain of education leads to corruption in every other arena of culture. People take whatever they learn, know and embrace as truth (even if it's a lie) and sow it wherever they go.

A corrupt government begins with a corrupt education. It's time for God's glory to invade hearts and the heart of academia.

IT'S TIME TO RECLAIM A WISE EDUCATION

> WISE AND KNOWLEDGE-ABLE LEADERS BRING STABILITY TO A NATION.

God is building His house on earth; He is training us to be skilled workers in our assignments from Him. Our children don't need to wait until they are forty to learn about their Kingdom assignments and skills needed. They are to be trained to think that way now!

In this present move of God, our talents, gifts, and abilities (both natural and spiritual) are going to function with a fresh Spirit of wisdom that will release God's glory through our gifts and skills. I pray that you grasp this for you and your children, your grandchildren, your nephews and nieces, or any children you teach or influence!

There is now a fresh empowering in natural and spiritual abilities as Holy Spirit visits His people with fresh revelation to understand issues and discover wise solutions. In the Old Testament, Joshua led Israel into their promised inheritance because he had a *spirit of wisdom* (Deut. 34:9). His leadership skills were not only well developed, but he was also a man of God's presence.

A new wave of wise education is now needed for this generation. We must prepare the children for their place of blessing in the world and for advancing Father's Kingdom.

The old Humanistic way has failed and is crumbling beneath its own weight. Our nation today is desperate for people wise and skilled on every mountain of culture. If we are to advance as a nation, we must reclaim this mountain and its gates.

There is a new movement of parents and teachers now seeking fresh solutions for the children. Reformation is on the horizon to empower parents to see their children's gifts and divine purpose. There is fresh wave of wisdom coming for the younger generation who will rise bold as lions in their Kingdom assignments. We must train them for this.

Here are a few ways you can stand at the gate of education:

- Decree this mountain to be set free into God's original design for it.
- Pray for revival and the outpouring of God's glory in education halls!
- Pray for repentance of ungodly decisions made in the school systems. Pray for wisdom and boldness for teachers and the students to stand for righteousness.

- Discern if the education being given is sound wisdom and truth. If not, speak up.
- Ask the Holy Spirit for creative strategies and solutions that advance good education. Perhaps write or suggest good curriculums / supplements for schools.
- Vote for righteous educational leaders; intercede for those in seats of educational authority to stand strong against evil agendas and act with wisdom and love for the children's well-being and future.
- Speak up for parental rights.
- Attend PTA meetings and school board meetings; hold school boards accountable.
- Research what books are allowed in your child's school library.

Pray with me: *Father, You see the assault on today's education and those who prey on the young. Send in the light bearers! I ask that You turn this tide of evil! I ask for mercy and justice for the seed of this nation. Use me to help bring a cultural shift for a right and wise education that the children might thrive in the light the way You intend. They don't deserve the tyranny of darkness and false enlightenment. They are Yours. In Jesus' name. Amen.*

To Ponder:

- *How are you furthering your own education for your life?*

8

THE FATHER'S HEART FOR COMMERCE

"I will abundantly bless her provision;
I will satisfy her needy with bread." – Psalm 132:15

In the book of Revelation we read of the heavenly Jerusalem having streets of gold and foundation stones of costly gems (Rev. 21:19-21). God is not poor, and poverty is not His standard of piety. Neither is wealth the evidence of godliness, but God delights to see us prosper. Fruitfulness and increase bring Him glory.

As a good Father, He delights to provide for us, including prospering us through the work of our hands.

In the Scripture above, we see His promise *and desire* to satisfy our needs. He is not stingy, nor holds back any good thing from us. He loves us. He wants us to flourish. He not only provides for us but teaches us to increase through business. Business (commerce) is the trade route of provision, and provision brings peace, security, and stability.

Godly commerce is part of God's ways.

GODLY
COMMERCE
IS
PART OF
GOD'S
WAYS.

Every one of us has a role on the mountain of commerce, whether as a consumer, employee, entrepreneur, or CEO. Business empowers the financial well-being of a family and a nation. Father wants individuals, families and nations to prosper in their labor.

The mountain of commerce involves the realm where ideas become inventions and where products and services are created and exchanged for money, or for barter. It is the marketplace of goods, amenities, investments and where careers take shape. It is the wheel of industrial growth and technological advancement.

It is the place where the river of currency flows, and where wealth is made and shared.

Commerce is the place where we are able to create wealth to have our needs met *and* to empower us for giving benevolently – it is where sufficiency and abundance are gained.

One of God's names is El Shaddai – the All Sufficient One, the God who is more than enough, the One who does for us what we cannot do for ourselves. When we do not know what to do, we can call on His name, *El Shaddai*. He will both provide and teach us what we need to do to prosper.

Wealth and prosperity are intended by God to be a *minister* of His goodness to us, to our families, and to this world.

The world of business and trade are meant to be a beautiful and righteous benefit for the provider, seller, and buyer of goods that brings sufficiency where there is lack and provision where there is need.

THE BLESSING WITHIN COMMERCE

Proverbs 10:22 says *the blessing of the Lord makes one rich (brings wealth)*. God's blessing is a spiritual dynamic that manifests in unlimited ways, both spiritual and natural. Blessings originate in God who blesses us so that we, in turn, can *be* a blessing. This blessing includes the realms of business and finances.

This means that the nature of business and finance carry a **spiritual component.** This realm of culture is rich with God-given capacities designed to bring growth, provision, and wealth. Commerce is purposed by God to function with His love and glory in every process – from the boardroom to manufacturing to employment to distribution.

According to Beverley Watkins and Robert Henderson in their book, *The Trading Floors of Heaven*, "Trading is integral to God's desire to see His kingdom established on earth as it is in heaven."[1]

As we saw earlier in the parable of the talents, commerce is the tool of heaven to bring increase to His Kingdom. **Increase is part of the Genesis mandate and is infused into all of God's ways.** Wherever God's glory dwells, it brings increase.

> INCREASE IS THE DNA OF GOD'S GLORY.

Isaiah 9:7 says that the government of His Son is *ever increasing*. Romans 1:17 says we go from *faith to faith*. 2 Corinthians 3:18 teaches that our transformation is from *glory to glory*, and Proverbs 4:18 tells us that the path of the just shines *brighter and brighter* until the perfect day. Even the universe, since the day of its creation, is said by scientists to *still be expanding*.

These reveal God's desire for us, as His image, to *increase in every way*. **Increase is the DNA of God's glory**. It is the nature of His unlimited measure operating through the law of fruitfulness and multiplication – manifesting His Kingdom that moves in ever increasing movement.

This includes finances and using our abilities to create products and services for our benefit and the blessing of others. There is divine reward for *Godly* stewardship in these matters, beyond what we know.

GUARDING THE GATES OF INCREASE

Every person, family, community and nation need a strong economy for flourishing. Good laws and businesses structures that prosper trade are core to a strong personal and national economy. Businesses are a gift and blessing from God. We need to pray for businesses to succeed righteously.

As God's image-bearers our prosperity is never to be for selfish reasons. Rather, it is given for personal needs, to help finance Kingdom assignments, help the poor, and empower us as ministers of His goodness to others. **He wants our communities and nations to prosper as a mirror of heaven.** There is no lack or poverty in heaven.

I call those who operate in business or trade as *trade specialists*. This includes entrepreneurs, business owners, inventors, designers, doctors and technicians. It includes builders, financial investors and accountants, farmers, and the vast array of suppliers of goods and services of all kinds. These are also gatekeepers.

GOD GIVES US POWER FOR INCREASE.

Deuteronomy 8:18 says, *"He gives us power to make wealth."* That word *"power"* includes *strength of mind, empowered capacities, and the ability to shift in new ways.* In times like what we are experiencing now, we need the ability to shift in new ways of doing business, and of creating new paths of provision. We need fresh trade routes and new inventions. It is not an option. It's time to access blueprints and strategies that are in the glory waiting for us to discover!

God *"gives"* us power for increase! The word **gives** (Heb. *natan*) means: **to appoint, assign, designate.** Father has assigned us to prosper! *"Making wealth"* means: *to produce, acquire, or fashion riches, resources, or armed forces.* No family or army succeeds without resources and finances. We are the family *and* the army of the Lord; wealth acuteness is essential.

Eden itself watered lands of gold.

Trading and commerce are not an invention of man, but was happening in heaven long ago. Since business comes from God, I don't think it is wrong to say that God is a "Business Man." He has an expectation of reward for what He sows and for what He labors.

God is the source of witty inventions, new products, and needed services. He rains His ideas on the righteous and unrighteous because He loves this world. He wants us to come up higher, see fresh business blueprints in His glory like Moses saw, and manifest them on earth.

As I've shared, the Genesis mandate was about **stewardship** and **increase** – the same as in the parable of the ten talents. Jesus said He was to be about His Father's "business." *We* are the Father's business, and the great return on His investment is *many* sons and daughters of glory who cover the earth with His radiance. This includes His glory in commerce!

In commerce, some excel to become giants in trade like Sam Walton (founder of Walmart), David Green (founder of Hobby Lobby), or Warren Buffet (an investment strategist). Others succeed in business as "thought leaders" like author John Maxwell or Earl Nightingale. Others may not have big names but their services are equally important. The ways of business and commerce are limitless – from mom-and-pop shops, to mega corporations, to everything in between.

The business world carries a huge influence in culture. No wonder Satan has seduced many corporations today to use their influence to promote ungodliness and evil in culture. Corporation leaders need the light of God for their businesses to function as Father intends.

Many have reached incredible heights of wealth but are funding the kingdom of darkness with their treasures. Without discernment, many on this mountain are following a lead of corrupt ethics and even demonic agendas in commerce.

We need Father's light-bearers to rise in business!

THE SPIRIT OF UNDERSTANDING

As God's image bearers, He wants us to not only succeed in business, but to pray for the businesses of our cities. Without strong business, families suffer and communities decline. We see this in cities where factories move away or close down, and once thriving communities become ghost towns. Many businesses fail because of internal problems such as poor management, lack of sufficient finances, or poor business practices.

Others fail because of external factors, government control, heavy taxation, or disasters. And too, seasons change and businesses must continually shift, upgrade, and see the future to make needed adjustments and changes.

PROSPERING IS PART OF COVENANT PROMISE.

We must ask God for fresh blueprints and strategies from heaven. In the Old Testament, Isaac (Abraham's son) sowed in the land where God told him to dwell, and he prospered one-hundred-fold even in a time of famine! Father gave him the ability to prosper when every other market dried up. God can do amazing things with us if we follow His lead!

Prospering is part of covenant promise. Our prosperity, however, needs to be free from greed. Sufficiency and abundance are for us, but not about us. Rather, they are about the demonstration of Father's love as a provider to us *and* what is beyond ourselves.

All businesses need knowledge, wisdom, and understanding to thrive. These are found in the Holy Spirit!

The Hebrew word for **understanding** (*bina*) means: *the faculty of perfect understanding, insight, wisdom, and the ability to distinguish or judge a matter.* It speaks of an *internal ability to "connect the dots" with keen insight.* But what's more is that the **spirit of understanding** conveys the idea of a *"house of living revelation."* (Think about that!)

Isaac was a man in covenant with God and had revelation for prospering. God wants to give us revelation for increase.

In changing times, when commerce hits unforeseen walls in a turbulent world, we need more than our own wits. We need God. Thankfully, He is delighted to give us the revelation we need to succeed. He loves to gives us His *Spirit of understanding* to unlock in us an ability to increase and make wealth.

> GOD WANTS TO GIVE US REVELATION FOR INCREASE!

To succeed at anything takes training and fresh vision, as well as sacrifice. It requires endurance, patience, and insight.

God promises to give us power and understanding as we seek Him. He will give new revelation with the ability to distinguish the path before us for accessing new provision and blessing. Look for it, because God's glory will be poured out with ever increasing ways to prosper in days ahead. There are new strategic inventions, goods, services and solutions yet to be discovered.

PROSPERITY HAS PREDATORS

One of the predators on the mountain of commerce is a spirit nature that embodied Israel's ancient foe, the *"Canaanite."* *Canaanite* means: *merchant, trader, trafficker, and is linked with shame and humiliation.* This nature links with *spirits of pride, greed* and *Mammon* (wealth, materialism) at the expense and exploitation of others.

If our heart isn't kept right these spirits can easily influence us to align with ungodly agreements and business practices such as backroom deals, taking bribes, embezzlement, trafficking, and the exchange of money "under the table." They work to compromise ethics and integrity, using deceit and fraud for unjust gain. These are often found even behind the mask of philanthropy or government mandates made "for the good of the people" but have a hidden agenda.

In Amos chapter 8, the Lord warns against corruption in business that *skimps on measurements, boosts prices and cheats with dishonest scales.* God watches to see when people are taken advantage of, including what He calls *"selling the sweepings of the wheat."* This can refer to things added to products that make it appear "more" when it is simply junk filler, and actually contaminates the purity of a product.

God sees and will bring judgment on corrupt acts and those who engage them.

The great capacity for trade was a gift given to Lucifer in heaven before his fall. However, when pride entered his heart, it perverted his gift to greed and selfish ambition (Ezek. 28:14-16). His influence is at the root of corruption in business. James 3:16

says that envy and selfish-ambition is the open door to disorder and *every evil thing.*

Again, Nahum 3:4 gives us a clear description of Satan's trading described as *selling (trafficking) nations through immorality, and families (people groups) through witchcraft.*

Trafficking is the realm of stealing and exploiting something for reaping wealth through trade. It is a wealth made not from one's own product or service but on something stolen or exploited. This includes slavery, extortion, blackmail, unjust wages, and abuse of land. It also includes abortion, infanticide and human trafficking.

Statistics show that 24.9 million people are trafficked every year worldwide.[2] Some say it may be up to 40 million including slave labor, domestic servitude, and sex trafficking. According to Operation Unground Railroad, 2 million of the trafficked are children. It is one of the most terrible and lucrative businesses engaged globally and participated in by government officials, CEOs, clergy, and people of all walks. Meanwhile, the wicked fill their pockets with the profits of innocent blood and lives.

God will deal with the people and the systems that are using trade for evil and unjust gain. As ambassadors of heaven, we are to stand at this mountain-gate in prayer and with godly action that contends for righteousness in commerce.

Money is power and power easily corrupts. Those with a good understanding, however, see the end of the matter and will use caution to keep their heart right.

Father wants us to prosper in *godly ways* that brings benefit to the world around us! There are many who are coming into a new season of prosperity and fresh insight for business. There is coming a new wave of technology and ability to make wealth. There are fresh mantles being released for Godly commerce!

We need *holy trade specialists who move with the Spirit of the Son for communities to prosper.* Does your heart long to prosper in new ways? To excel in business? To bring new ideas into manifestation as products and services? If so, that is a gift of God.

Here are a few ways to stand at the gate of this mountain:

- Decree this mountain to be set free into God's glory and original design for it.

- Pray for a revival of righteousness in corporate policies and decisions. Pray for CEOs to move with the heart of the Father regarding their employees, wages, and practices that impact their employee's lives.

- Pray for divine strategies, blueprints, inventions, products and solutions that advance Father's provision and goodness through business endeavors.

- Ask Father for new business ideas and insights for prospering with many streams of income.

- Support those who are exposing evil trade schemes, such as human trafficking.

Pray with me: *Father, send in the light bearers to bring light to this sphere of culture! Let strongholds of darkness be broken off the agencies advancing the kingdom of darkness. Empower Your people like You did with Isaac to succeed in times of trouble. Help me to do what's right in every aspect of business or trade. Help me to support Your ways for this sphere of culture. I love You. In Jesus' name. Amen.*

To Ponder:

- *Is there a business idea that God has given you that is still sitting on a shelf?*

- *Are you believing God for increase? If not, why?*

9

THE FATHER'S HEART FOR FAMILY

"He will turn the hearts of the fathers back to their children and the hearts of the children to their fathers so that I will not come and strike the land with complete destruction." – Malachi 4:6

The health of a nation is reflected in the health of the family bond. According to the above Scripture, a nation's rise or ruin hinges on the heart condition between parents and children.

For God's glory to be revealed in our nation, the heart of the family must be restored.

From Genesis to Revelation God reveals His heart to us through family concepts and speaks to us in family terms. He relates to us in the context of our identity as His sons and daughters. God is our Father and Jesus is His Son; the Son is building the Father's house. Jesus is also our Elder Brother and we are brothers and sisters in Him. The Holy Spirit is our Comforter, Helper, and Teacher, and the Church is a *Bride* to Christ, the Anointed One.

The strength of the parent-child relationship is not only the strength of a nation, but is the foundation of our personal life and development. Families are the building blocks of nations, since nations themselves are families. As they say, *"So goes the family, so goes the nation."*

Every mountain of culture directly impacts the well-being of the family from government to business to education to the arts and entertainment to media. All mountains are meant by God to support the well-being of the family.

God takes note of how each mountain of influence supports or opposes His design for marriages and the family. This is important as we labor on every other mountain: *how does what I do impact the well-being of my marriage, family, and my children. How do my decisions impact and the well-being of the families of my nation?*

Does my life, work decisions and activities support or oppose God's designs for family? How do the laws I vote for and the corporate ethics I support impact the Father's desires for families? Are they life-giving, or are they life-taking?

WE ARE TO LOVE PEOPLE, BUT DISCERN THE SPIRIT BEHIND AGENDAS.

A recent example of a negative impact on family from the entertainment mountain would be Disney's vow to promote an LGBT agenda through their movies. That agenda opposes God's heart and design for individuals and families. We are to love people but discern the spirit behind agendas.

OUR NEED FOR COMMUNITY

Every human being was created with a core need for family and community. We have a deep need to belong. We didn't come into this world through an isolated event, but through the union of two other people and the womb of our mother. Our genetics come from those who came before us. As little children, we couldn't have survived on our own.

Research shows that if a baby is left alone without being touched it will die, even if fed.[1] Documented studies show that those who survive their first years without sufficient touch or being held can suffer a lack in proper brain development.[2]

We were created with a need for interaction with others. We need people committed to us in a mutual bond of love, especially in our early developmental stages. We need strong and loving relationships all through our lives.

As human beings we have specific core needs, including: **community, personal worth, structure, security, stimulation, validation, and spirituality.** These core needs are God-given and are intended by Him to be met first within the family when we are young. However, we know that circumstances can hinder that structure, whether by illness, absence, or death of a parent, or abuse.

When these core needs are met in a healthy bond of love, it roots the heart in confidence and a sense of deep personal worth and belonging. When those needs are not met, it can create deep inner turmoil regarding our sense of identity, worth, and purpose.

As we age and grow in Christ, we learn to find our needs met by God as our first source of love and truth in these matters. He is able to supply whatever has been lost or missing in our lives.

THE FAMILY BOND

God's family framework is designed so that each individual flourishes in every way. Each one is to be valued and respected. In God's family design parents serve through leadership, love, protection, and nurturing care. Children serve through honor and obedience. Each person carries a significant part and value to the whole family.

Let's look at some of these valuable roles.

1 – MARRIAGE

God's design begins with the marriage of a **man and woman**, the *"two becoming one"* in a marriage covenant. A covenant is an oath of protection and provision where each one gives their all for the other. Covenants involve words and vows. They are spiritual in nature as each one shares not just themselves, but spiritual alignments they carry into that bond (Selah). This bond is reinforced through physical intimacy.

LOVE IS THE POWER BY WHICH WE THRIVE!

God established the man to be the *head* of the marriage and home. The *head* (Grk. *Kephale*) means: *source of life*. The head carries a preeminence and an authority for the well-being of everything under its care (1 Cor. 11:3). Just naturally speaking, without a head you have no life or strength.

However, God also says that the husband has a head – Christ, whose head is the Father. This cycle of dynamic life flow from the Father to Jesus to a husband to a wife is meant to empower each one, as well as the generations produced through a *love covenant cycle*.

Love is the power by which we thrive. This makes the role of a husband prominent in nurturing the heart of his wife, causing her to flourish in the marriage. This is the picture of what Jesus' love does for us. It's why the Apostle Paul said, *"Men, love your wives as Christ loved the Church"* (Eph. 5:25).

Paul also said that wives are to *submit to their husband*, **though never as to force or abuse**. Rather, it is to be a cooperation to someone who loves them. This, too, is a picture of our life with Jesus as His Bride (His Church).

In my book, *The Empowered Woman*, I go into more detail regarding God's designs for marriage. There has been a lot of abuse in Christian marriages because of misinterpretations of Scripture. Knowing the truth sets us free and empowers marriages to operate in love and honor as God designed it.

2 – THE IMPORTANCE OF THE FATHER

There is no greater need in America today than the restoration of fathers and families. Currently there are approximately 18.3 million American children (1 in 4) living without a father in the home. Sadly, the U.S. has the highest rate of children in the world living in a single-parent home, with 80 percent of those homes led by single mothers. America is now the most *fatherless* nation in the world.

According to a Rasmussen poll taken in January of 2022, 84% of Americans believe a strong family is foundational to a strong America.[3] God designed the father to be the strength of the family, which in turn strengthens a nation.

This is reflected in the very Hebrew word for *father* (*av*) that means: the *strength or leader of the home*. There is strength and power not just in a man's physical body, but in his love as a home builder. A father's love, labor and blessing are the strength of a home. His love not only enriches his wife, but roots the **hearts** of his children in a deep sense of security and identity.

The very Hebrew word for *love* (*ahav*) means: *behold the father*, or *the heart of the father revealed*. A father's heart filled with love is the strength of the home.

True love creates an atmosphere of joy and affirmation. Love makes you feel like you belong, like you fit, and you are valued.

Another strength a father provides is wise counsel. The word *counsel* (Heb. *esa*) means: *to advise, give purpose, and by implication give a plan for achieving success of something.* Fatherly counsel is part of caring for a child – of seeing their destiny and encouraging their development and vision for a purpose-filled future.

One of the greatest strengths a child receives from a father is his verbal blessing. A father's blessing carries a spiritual force that empowers the peace, prosperity and destiny of his child. It's why Jesus wanted the children to come to Him – so He could bless their destiny.

The opposite is also true – a father's curse carries life impacting negative patterns in a child's heart and mind about themselves. A cursed child will curse his own destiny.

Can you see how important a father's role is in the home? If you have not been blessed by your father, know that the Heavenly Father has released this over you through Jesus. Take a moment to read the covenant blessings of God for you in Deuteronomy 28:1-14.

I don't think most men realize the strength and influence the sound of their voice carries, or what weight their opinions have on the heart of their wives and children.

This is why God calls the hearts of men to first know His love, be rooted and filled with His love, and be the giver of love in their homes. Families need fathers to be home in both heart and in presence. Just look at the Hebrew word for *anger* (Heb. *ayav*) that means: *where is the father?*

Our nation is filled with angry children – young and old – longing for the love, presence, and affirmation of their father. A father's love is demonstrated through his involvement, guidance, and good counsel. Many men don't feel like they have anything to offer, but they do! America needs the hearts of men to be healed and bring that healing home. God has mantled men in a unique way that is needed for the healing of our families and nation. We must pray for fathers.

In counseling I see many Christians who struggle in their identity and relationship with the Heavenly Father – a struggle most often rooted in a broken relationship with an earthly father. How a father interacts with us (or not) creates a filter of how we tend to see God as our Father. It shapes our sense of worth and belonging, even in our relationship to Him.

> THE HEAVENLY FATHER WANTS TO HEAL OUR HEARTS AND BE KNOWN AS A GOOD FATHER, BECAUSE HE IS.

The Heavenly Father wants to heal our hearts and be known as a good Father, because He is. It's why Paul prayed that the saints would be rooted and grounded in His love. Abba Father's love is the source of our life, strength, and identity as His children.

In Psalm 27:10, David said, "*When my father and my mother forsake [neglect, abandon] me, then the Lord will take care of me.*" David knew the rejection of a father. He also experienced Abba Father's healing love, counsel, and embrace.

I have seen God heal many hearts through a deep encounter with His Fathering love.

The same principle applies for the need of a mother's kindness and comfort. Many have been deeply hurt by the abandonment or abuse by a mother, whether physical or verbal. God, whose heart is also mothering, is able to heal those wounds as well.

3 – THE IMPORTANCE OF A MOTHER

The word for *mother* (Heb. *em*) means: *first or strong water*. It conveys the idea of water providing refreshing and nourishing.

In Scripture, words are said to be like water. A mother's words and touch are intended by God to bring comfort and nurturing for children to grow strong.

The Hebrew word for *fear* (*terror, dread*) is *eyma* and means: **what happens when there is no mother.** It speaks of what happens when there is no one to speak kindly with words of comfort, encouragement, or truth to counter whatever is putting us in dread.

Mothers also carry an important role in the life of a child through words and touch that are meant to comfort and fortify.

As with a father, how our mothers have interacted with us also impacts our development. Were our mother's words and actions encouraging or discouraging? Were they kind or did they tear us down? Words are powerful, especially when they come from the one designed to impart faith, hope, and truth. God wants to heal us of any "mother wounds." He is well able to do that. I know this to be true.

I have written about the power of God to heal our hearts from family troubles in my book, *Life with Abba Father*. It includes my own healing journey.

4 – THE IMPORTANCE OF A CHILD

Psalm 127:3 describes children as a gift to parents and a parents' inheritance. Children create a legacy to their name. The Hebrew word for *son* (*ben*) means: **builder of the house**, and *daughter* (*bat*) is the **covenant sign of the house**.

This parent-child relationship is meant to be one of love, sacrifice and honor for each other. Parents sacrifice for the well-being of their children. In turn, children are to honor their parents as those who God used to give them life (Deut. 5:16). That honor releases divine blessing for their life and future.

God's blueprint for family has no room for narcissism. Anywhere. It is a covenant bond where each one is to be honored, served, and valued.

Are you seeing the beauty of how God designed the family to function? Each one is to be blessed and to be a blessing. When this cycle of love and unity is honored, the generations become a powerful force of good in the earth. Where disrespect, dishonor, and disunity exist, a force of evil is released. It's why Satan works to tear apart the family so a force of evil is released.

> EACH MEMBER OF THE FAMILY SHOULD BE HIGHLY VALUED THROUGH WORDS AND ACTIONS.

If the earthly family is to mirror God's design, each member should be highly valued through words and actions that demonstrate blessing and commitment. When a marriage covenant is broken, so are hearts. Each one suffers. Men and women suffer. Children suffer.

To heal the heart of the family, we must heal the heart of the individuals within the family through forgiveness, love, and truth. Young and old alike need to feel loved and blessed by their family. Where that isn't possible, God will meet our needs and bring others to restore what has been stolen by the devil.

Remember, people are not our enemy – principalities, powers, and works of darkness are. God's light and truth will go to the core issues and restore life to our inner-being if we ask Him.

BREAKDOWN IN THE FAMILY

When love and nurturing is absent, or abuse is present, its ill effects can last a life time in the heart of an individual, no matter how old they are. Such soul wounds left unhealed can hinder a person's full development in how they view themselves and the world around them. It can impact the development of their gifts, relationships, and purpose.

According to psychology specialists, three million children are mistreated in the U.S. every year. 70 percent of this number are neglected, nearly 20 percent are physically abused, and 12 percent are sexually abused. Maltreatment of a child wreaks havoc on their emotional and physical state of being. This can impact a person's ability to rightly bond with others. In psychology, it is called "attachment disorder."

Psychologists at Evergreen Psychotherapy Center write, "Attachment disorder is transmitted intergenerationally. Children lacking secure attachments with caregivers commonly grow up to be parents who are incapable of establishing this crucial foundation with their own children. Instead of following the instinct to protect, nurture and love their children, they abuse, neglect and abandon them. The situation today is out of control. Consider the following:[4]

- 81% of child victims were maltreated by a parent acting alone or with someone else.

- The youngest children are most vulnerable; those under one had the highest rates of abuse; almost 50% of all child fatalities caused by maltreatment were under one year of age.

- Up to 65% of maltreated children develop PTSD; as many as 90% of infants and children acquire anxious and disorganized attachment patterns.

- Maltreated children are 53% more likely to be arrested as a juvenile and 40% more likely to commit a violent crime.

- 50 to 80% of all child abuse cases involve drug and/or alcohol abuse by parents or caregivers.

- Children of families in poverty were 45 times more likely to suffer neglect and 60 times more likely to die from maltreatment.

- The fiscal cost of childhood maltreatment, including mental health, medical, social services, and justice system services, is estimated at $104 billion per year."

Recently, our local news related that in 2021 there were more than 27,000 cases of abuse reported in Dallas County, Texas.[5] That is just one county among 254 counties in Texas, and that number only reflects what was reported.

That means 27,000 imprints of fear, trauma, and terror most often by the hands of those who should be ministers of good and love to those children. It is heart rending to think about.

Unfortunately, these imprints don't just go away with age. They grow with you and manifest as low self-esteem, neediness, inability to deal with stress or adversity, or maintain friendships. **It can include feelings of alienation, aggression, a lack of empathy, or inability to perceive truth. These are just a few of how trauma impacts the soul's formation.**

There is no greater need in America today than the healing of the family. Father wants to heal every child, young person, and adult with His love.

Guarding the Family Gate

The first gatekeeper of family is the husband and father. After all, he is the head and initiator of the covenant marriage and family. Next to him is the wife and mother who has her key role, too, as a keeper of covenant love. They are the gatekeepers of their marriage and of their children's destinies.

We watch in horror the school shootings, abductions, death by family members, and rise in human trafficking and suicide.

Yet many still approve of a mother destroying a baby inside the womb. To stop the spirit of murder in our nation, we must stop it at the gate of a mother's womb. To stop the mental health crisis in our nation we must stop the emotional bleeding in the hearts of family members.

One of the tenets of communism that came into America decades ago came with the very intention to bring America down by abolishing the traditional family structure.[6] An anti-family agenda is an anti-Christ (and anti-Father) spirit that works through agendas such as abortion, infanticide, welfare systems supporting the absence of a father from the home, and the pornography industry. It includes Planned Parenthood, Antifa, LGBTQ⁺ agendas, and the transgender movement. These all target the destruction of the family.

Restoring the family begins by taking back the truth of our creation out of the lying hands of Darwinism and out from the tyranny of Humanism and Socialism that are choking the destiny of babies and families.

KICKING THE PREDATOR OUT THE DOOR

These assaults on family are nothing less than spiritual warfare. One that we must understand. One of Israel's ancient enemies was the *Jebusites*. It was a spiritual enemy that we still face today. *Jebusite* means: *threshing floor, to trample, to reject, kick out.*

Like other tribes of Canaan, the Jebusites worshiped many gods including Tessub, the weather god,[7] and Sauska, also known as **Ishtar** – the goddess of love and war and **protector of prostitutes and patroness of the brothel**. The worship of Ishtar promotes the delight of bodily love apart from covenant. Ishtar also has many names in different cultures – in Babylon she was known as Astarte, in pagan Europe she was known as Eastre or *Easter*.[8]

These gods and goddesses are not myths but principalities. They seek to destroy the family bond through "stormy" conflicts, immorality, pornography, and unfaithfulness. They work to trample the heart and soul of family members through abuse, rejection, and divorce.

We are meant to experience faithful love, honor and blessing in family relationships, but sin and soul wounds passed from generation to generation have created terrible brokenness, abandonment, and trauma in a vast majority. Self-rejection, lack of connection, and a sense of worthlessness are just a few of the results of how the enemy works to destroy lives.

> IT'S TIME TO KNOW WHO WE ARE AND OUR TRUE PURPOSE ON EARTH.

These works of darkness spawn co-dependencies, ungodly soul ties, and twisted gender pursuits looking for love and acceptance in all the wrong places. These have replicated unimaginable patterns of self-destructive behavior in lives and culture.

America is in an identity crisis because the American family is in an identity crisis.

The American family is in an identity crisis because God's own family has been in an identity crisis of not truly knowing who we are and why we are here.

It's time to know who we are and our true purpose on earth. It's time to understand our mantle of Kingdom identity for healing individuals, families, and nations.

In this end-time harvest movement, there is a fresh awakening for the restoration of the family as we read in Malachi 4:6. Revival and reformation is starting in God's own household as He brings the prodigals back home and rebuilds our homes to mirror heaven. More and more ministries are beginning to focus on how to help marriages heal and how parents can better love and nurture their children in love and righteousness.

This will take repentance of narcissism in the hearts of everyone, including parents and children. As the family unit begins to heal, we will see the healing of our nation, and it begins with healing our own relationship with Abba Father.

Here are a few ways to stand with the Father and Jesus at the gate of this mountain:

- Decree a righteous return to Godly family foundations and for families to be set free into the Father's love.

- Ask God to heal any wound in your own heart from broken family relationships.

- Pray for a revival of God's original designs for family. Stand against ideologies that tear that covenant pattern apart.

- Pray for a return of the heart of parents and children, for men and women to know their true identity and value and be fully present for their family.

- Pray for strategies and solutions on how you can help strengthen families through spiritual parenting / mentoring / counselling.

- Hold social services and foster agencies accountable for the lives they are touching – some have been involved in child trafficking.

- Support the pro-life movement and movements that restore family relationships.

Pray with me: *Father, bring Your light and love to heal men, women, and children from all the destruction that darkness has brought into our* homes. Stop the waters of hell and loose the waters of heaven to restore and renew the American family. Heal each heart, restore true identity and value to every individual. Heal every emotional wound and physical bruise. Heal the broken bones of family unity. In Jesus' name. Amen.

To Ponder:

- Do you feel a leading from God to make an impact in this area of culture? If so, in what way?

10

THE FATHER'S HEART FOR MEDIA

"How delightful on the mountains are the feet of one who brings good news, who announces peace and brings good news of happiness, who announces salvation, and says to Zion, 'Your God reigns!'" – Isaiah 52:7

I t is said that nothing happens or changes unless someone says something. It is a creation principle ... *God said*, and it was so.

As God's likeness, our words also carry power to create and influence change, whether spoken or written. This makes the mountain of media a *power house* and key player of cultural influence.

This also means that all communication at its core is **spiritual in nature**. This is why words carry such tremendous power.

Proverbs 18:21 says, **"Death and life are in the power of the tongue."** Since words are spiritual in nature, we must pay attention to the *intent* and spirit behind what is being communicated.

As God is the author of communication, it means that all its forms – written, spoken, digital, or broadcast – are to carry His heart and purposes. At creation, He set the standard for all communication as being the means for creating and empowering life.

Every conveyer of words is answerable to Him for what they say. (Selah – think about that!)

"But I tell you that for every careless word that people speak [words that do not produce life], they will give an account of it on the day of judgment" (Matt. 12:36).

This shows us that the Father's design *for media* is to release life and glory through messages that empower faith, hope, and love – words that are truth and inspire peace and joy.

UNDERSTANDING THE POWER OF WORDS

According to the law of first mention in biblical study, the first words spoken by God in Genesis 1 caused the light of His glory to manifest from the unseen realm into the seen realm. All succeeding created works came forth through continued divine declarations – all in the presence of His manifest glory on earth. For this reason, only His *glory-carriers* could rightly steward His glory works.

Research shows that all of creation responds to mankind's voice – from plants to animals, to water, to weather, and to spirits. As the redeemed, we have authority and influence over all these[1].

If you have never read the book *The Miracle of Water* by Masaru Emoto,[2] it is a powerful study regarding the impact of words – spoken and written – on anything composed of water.

All living things have water in them to one degree or another. You and I are 75% water.

It is no wonder that creation responds to words since it was made by words. Words are frequencies. Frequencies have cycles that set things in motion. These frequencies move and motivate us, whether words spoken by others or ourselves, including internal self-talk. Words can move us to excitement or to passivity; to flight, to fight, or to freeze.

Research proves that words carry frequencies that can alter neurological patterns, including our perspectives. They can create alternative patterns of thought and emotion, whether of love, hope, fear, resentment, and more.

> WORDS CAN MOVE US TO EXCITEMENT OR TO PASSIVITY.

Words create an experience. They produce emotions and emotions motivate behavior. Words can ignite, advance, or hinder events.

What comes from the mouth of media carries the greatest impact to shape cultural beliefs, ideologies, behaviors and the very atmosphere of a nation. That atmosphere can be heaven or hell.

Every other mountain of culture uses media to share their ideas, convey their information, and impress their messages on society. Gatekeepers on this mountain include: journalists, authors, news broadcasters, writers, historians, speakers and all who play a role in sharing information. This includes: books, publications, radio, television, podcasts, marketing, and the like.

As stewards of the earth, we are to be vigilant with what we hear and what we speak. What is the information that media is feeding society, or that we are listening to and accepting? Is it truth? Is it hopeful? Is it biased? Is it driving a narrative that is intentionally programming our behavior with a hidden agenda?

Words can be "spoken" in picture form too. As the saying goes – *pictures talk*. Think about the last time you suddenly got hungry as you watched a food commercial! It was telling you that you were hungry, even if you weren't! Why do you think QVC (quality-value-convenience) online shopping is so popular? They know the power of their words and demos to move you to give them your credit card number!

WORDS HAVE ASSIGNMENTS

According to Isaiah 55:11 we see that **words have assignments**; *"So also will be the word that I speak; it does not return to Me unfulfilled. My word performs My purpose and fulfills the mission I sent it out to accomplish" (TPT).* This is a spiritual law that applies to our words, too. It's the spiritual law by which we reap what we sow with our words.

Those in media know that what they say and how they say it has the ability to create change in public opinion. There is a psychology to getting people's attention. It's called marketing psychology. Political ads, medical ads, business ads all use this power.

Media is a seed to harvest tool. The question is, does the harvest they desire carry the Father's heart for life? Is the seed of their words life-giving? Is it moving us towards God's purposes, or away from them? What perspective is it fueling?

People today are desperate for words of life. American culture is reeling from being fed the death messages of wokeness. During the 2020 COVID pandemic a lot of Americans turned off their nightly news because it was being driven by dark agendas and hopeless narratives. It was making society sick in our soul.

Today, *woke* messaging is even being marketed on cereal boxes for children! Recently, Kellogg's ® came out with a new cereal for kids called *All Together*®. On the side of the box, it lists gender pronouns of he/him, she/her, and they/them and then encourages you to add your own gender pronouns. Rather than empowering children with truth of their identity, they are being told to make their identity whatever they want. It is the path of a perverse identity.

Identity, however, is already laced in them – they just need to know the truth about it and celebrate who God made them to be!

I find the name of that cereal interesting. God Himself is calling His people to a fresh unity. The LGBTQ+ agenda, however, is a counterfeit unity that springs from an unclean spirit. Satan always operates in counterfeit measure to what God is doing by creating a twisted narrative, as he did in Eden.

GUARDING THE GATES WITH TRUTH

America's strength as a nation in past generations was empowered through integrity, which was supported in media. Truth was a standard in culture. American broadcasting was reliable and you could trust what was said. It created a sense of security in what you were told. There were healthy standards of communication and curse words were censored.

People's words could be trusted as truth because they were. It is not so today. Unfortunately, many still believe what the media says about everything.

We were a strong nation, because we were a nation of truth. Truth empowers the *spirit of might* and courage. The Hebrew word for **might** (*gebura*) means: *strength, valor, might, bravery, mastery, force, mighty deeds*. For America to be strong again we must return to being a people of truth.

The lack of truth in media today has promoted a fearful and unstable cultural atmosphere. The media information highway is being filled with the data smog of misinformation, wrong information, and wicked propaganda. This messaging is creating anxiety and depression in people's lives rather than empowering life and hope.

People are struggling to know what is true, even in the circles we should be able to trust. Meanwhile, suicide rates among youth are surging as the security in their identity is being wrecked by lies, unhealthy social media, and woke culture. To add to this cultural dilemma is the suppression of truth.

Suppression of truth, along with spreading of lies, creates a weak people.

TRUTH NURTURES OUR BOND WITH GOD, WHILE LIES KEEP US FAR FROM GOD.

A Hebrew word for a *lie (kahas)* means: *to deceive, disappoint, swear falsely, fail.*[3] This word expresses the idea: **to hide the chamber of destruction.** In other words, a lie is occultic in nature, hiding the destruction within it. A lie will cause us to fail. It leads to disappointment and hope deferred.

America is in a media crisis because America is in a truth crisis. America needs a revival of truth that can only come through a return to God who is Truth.

Truth is meant to be the banner on the mountain of media so that its influence fills culture with glory, serving Father's purposes, and not Satan's. As we saw earlier, truth nurtures our bond with God, while lies keep us far from God. A nation filled with lies is a nation separated from God.

DISCERNING THE ADVERSARY

One of the enemies to this mountain is the ancient spirit that was behind Israel's enemy called the *"Girgashites."* Some sources believe they were giants. "Girgashite" has two meanings. The first meaning is *"one who turns back from a pilgrimage"* and the second meaning is *"dweller in clay soil or black mud."*[4]

Clay is weak material; *its inherent nature is to conform through pressing.* To have "feet of clay" refers to *being weak minded and governed by fears, doubts, and negativism.*

To be a dweller of clay is a place of instability. It speaks of a life shaped by the pressures of worldly messages and cultural conformity. We often talk about "peer pressure" but the world is not our peer. We are not of this world.

Satan uses communication highways laced with illusion and falsehood to shape our thoughts with fear and an unsound mind. The devil wants us to dwell in the murk of anxiety. The *pressures* of fear and oppression will cause us to stop advancing, and even turn back from the direction God has for us.

Scripture says we were made from clay, but our formation is to be by the hand of God, the Heavenly Potter, who shapes us in courage and truth for advancing in His love and divine purpose. In fellowship with Him, we become dwellers in glory ... not mud.

As light bearers, we are here to support Father's heart for society; we must lovingly and boldly speak life and write truth. God is now raising up new voices to further His Kingdom on all fronts of culture, including media. In days past, most Christians were part of a "silent majority." That time is over.

Many are learning to write books or find others to help them get the message in them out. New magazines and podcasts heralding truth are appearing. We are in an hour of the "roar" of the Lion of Judah and we need all-hands-on deck to publish His good tidings with power!

Here are a few ways to stand at this mountain-gate:

- Decree strongholds over media to fall and for America's airwaves to be set free into God's original design for it.

- Pray for media to return to righteousness. Pray for a revival of truth in media.

- Pray for fresh strategies and solutions in how you can advance truth in media.
- Intercede for those who work in media for wisdom and discernment in what they do.
- Boldly hold those accountable for regulatory laws to be strong advocates for wholesome messaging.
- Speak up boldly to those who share false information.
- Take action with whatever media God is showing you to engage – if write, write! If it's to speak, then speak!

Pray with me: *Father, give us great boldness in this hour to stand for truth at this gate of culture! Show me where my part is so that this nation can be healed through Your love and truth. In Jesus' name. Amen.*

To Ponder:
- *Has God called you to make a difference in this area of culture?*
- *In what ways do you see how media has changed culture?*

11

THE FATHER'S HEART FOR ARTS & ENTERTAINMENT

"The Lord takes pleasure in all He has made!"
Psalm 104:31b (NLT)

There is no mountain more delightful than this one for displaying the glory of God through creative works. This is especially true when those works are inspired by Him.

This sphere of culture is meant to bring delight and pleasure. Revelation 4:11 says that *all creation exists by and for God's pleasure.* God made our senses to experience delight in something we see, hear, or even taste – created works that inspire the heart, thrill the soul, and move our emotions. He created our hearts and minds to be fascinated with beauty. After all, the angels in the throne room of heaven experience wonder continually!

I like to call this mountain the *beauty mountain.*

Years ago, the Lord woke me up in the middle of the night to pray for my nation, America. As I prayed, I felt Him ask what *we* should do. At first, I was taken aback at the fact that God would ask ME what WE should do! Then, without even thinking, I burst out, "Release the artisans!"

Creativity is God's gift of invitation to step into the arena of imagination, to partner with Him in bringing new and yet unseen beauty into the earth realm – to delight our mouth with good things, inspire joy and fresh perspectives through stimulating sounds and dynamic visuals. Anointed music especially is like an attendant for escorting your heart into intimate engagement with God.

> ALL CREATION EXISTS BY AND FOR GOD'S PLEASURE

Creativity includes all forms of celebration through a diverse range of activities in performing arts such as: painting, sculpting, music, sports, and games. It includes theater, cinema, and the culinary arts, as well as literary, applied graphics and fine arts, and more. These works can carry both intended messages of the artist, as well as messages unique to the beholder.

God Himself is an artist. Just look outside and see the immense beauty and diversity of His work on land, sea, and sky as far as the eye can see.

Listen to David's words in Psalm 19:1-3, *"The heavens tell of the glory of God; and their expanse declares the work of His hands. Day to day pours forth speech, and night to night reveals knowledge."*

The Father's desire for all creative works is to reveal the diversity of His own delights through various modes. As I mentioned earlier regarding Romans 1:20, God's invisible attributes, eternal power, and divine nature is clearly perceived in His creation. God is an artist. An artist's heart is revealed in what they create. The heart of God in His creation reveals His immense love and delight in what He creates. He also delights to bring us pleasure through it all! I don't know about you, but just looking at the ocean, marine life, the mountains, and birds all give me great delight!

THE POWER OF PICTURES

The arena of the arts is so vast. It is described as the *social arena where values and virtues are shared – shaping both personal and social mindsets.* The arts are able to purposefully stimulate an individual's thoughts, emotions, beliefs, or ideas through the senses, or for communicating ideas that may be political, spiritual, or philosophical in nature.

Humans are visual creatures. According to Albert Mehrabian, a well-known psychologist, *"70 to 93% of human communication is nonverbal. Visuals are concrete and are more easily remembered than even words."*[1]

Images carry the power to create scenes in the mind to take you to a different place of thought, to an expanded understanding, or realm of inspiration. However, images can also create an addiction, such as with porn, which has been proven to rewire the brain.

Art can create beauty or evil imaginations.

Images can improve our creative thinking by awakening the other parts of our brain. Art was especially used by ancient Greeks to help spread their ideas and philosophies throughout the world. They used literary works, musical arts, poetry, drama and more to shape the mindsets of nations.

UNITY OF THE ARTISANS

The work of a single artisan brings beauty, but when artisans unify — each one adding their unique sound or skill – they are able to create a powerful synergistic beauty. This includes symphonies, plays, team sports, and productions of any kind.

Those who keep the gates of this mountain includes musicians, singers, artists, craftsmen, chefs, film makers, athletes, fashion makers, writers, inventors, and the like.

ARTS AND THE REALMS OF JOY

Artistic expression can be solemn, thoughtful, or joyful. Joy itself is a core human need. God uses the arts to refresh our souls and bring delight. In Psalm 16:11 the psalmist describes God's presence as being full of joy. The apostle Paul also describes God's Kingdom as righteousness, peace, and *joy* in the Holy Spirit! (Rom. 14:17)

God is a joyful Father, He has a joyful Son, and a joy-filled Holy Spirit.

Many years ago, a minister told me that God doesn't care if we are happy. I believe he was wrong and that Father *does* care that we have an abundant life as Jesus said. That life includes joy. As a mother, I want my children to know joy. I want them to be responsible to do what is right *and* to also experience a life of joy.

How much more does our Father desire that for us?

The very first place where God put man was called **Eden,** which means: *pleasure, delight.* In Scripture we read that the joy of the Lord is our strength, and that a joyful heart is like good medicine for the soul and body (Neh. 8:10; Pro. 17:22). His Kingdom is righteousness, peace, and joy. Creative works bring us into the realms of joy!

I say all this because there are those who spend more time thinking that God is mad at them, rather than experiencing His delight in them and around them. Yet story after story in His Word displays His goodness towards us. God's own creative works tell us of a loving Sovereign who called everything He made "good." Creating humanity was God's pleasure. Mankind is still His delight. He is continuing to restore what He created in His image, and He uses the arts to prosper that restoration.

The arts are an important part of revival and reformation for conveying the heart and glory of God to culture.

THE ENEMY IS A SEDUCER OF SOULS

One of the enemies seeking to operate through artisans is the nature of the ancient "*Hivite.*" The name *Hivite* means: *villager, encampment, strong chamber*. It is also means *wicked*.

While we were created for community and good pleasure with godly imaginations that lift our spirits, the Hivite nature speaks of what partners with wicked spirits that dwells in the chambers of darkness. Their creative works are expressed through perverse and dark arts.

> CREATING HUMANITY WAS GOD'S PLEASURE. MANKIND IS STILL HIS DELIGHT.

Rather than inspire towards goodness, their works promote carnal and sensual pleasures through dark music, sexual perversions, and witchcraft. Their creations seduce the heart to connect the mind, will, and emotions with Hades through things that feel good but enchain the soul with bondage.

This spirit draws people into wrong associations and activities that make them think they are "living it up," all the while being escorted into strongholds of darkness.

The works of this enemy preys on humanity's base nature. It ensnares minds in addictions and releases demonic activity into people's lives through enticement and enchantment, taking people further into darkness than they ever intended to go. This is the opposite of the joy and life that God intends for us.

Years ago, the Church played a key role in keeping the gates of this mountain. There was a day when you couldn't say any bad word on television. There was a righteous censorship for the well-being of society. Unfortunately, when the Church stopped guarding this gate, the enemy quickly stepped in. We now see the devastation it has created in the soul of society.

It's time for the redeemed to return and stand at this gate.

THE SPIRIT OF HOLINESS

1 Chronicles 16:29 says, *"Oh, worship the Lord in the beauty of holiness!"* Our lives are meant to be a lifestyle of worship in everything we do, including the creative arts and entertainments we either create or engage.

Our gifts go to a whole new level of releasing the delight of God in the earth when the spirit we follow is the Holy Spirit in what we create.

There is a radiant freedom and pleasure in the holy realms for which we were created – realms from which we can draw amazing creativity that ministers life.

Holiness (Heb. *qodes*) means: ***what is sacred, sanctified, dedicated and set apart for God to host His abiding.*** It speaks of what is free from defilement. Holiness opens our eyes and spirit to see God (Heb. 12:14). Seeing Him is the well-spring for personal change and the ability to make Him known in unlimited and creative ways.

Today, God is raising up anointed artisans in every realm for releasing His glory and heart for humanity. One of my current favorite movies is the mini-series about Jesus and His disciples called *The Chosen*, a series produced by Dallas Jenkins. Wholesome entertainment draws the heart into the light and into well-being. People need hope, inspiration, and beauty. They need peace of soul.

Here are a few ways to stand at the gate of this mountain:

- Decree that the arts and entertainment industry be restored to God's original designs for them.

- Pray for those in this industry to be set free into God's love and purposes for their lives and work.

- Ask Holy Spirit for fresh inspiration and creative ideas for whatever area of arts and entertainment you are called to engage.

- Pray and intercede for the movie industry for repentance, cleansing, salvation, and deliverance. Pray for new producers and writers of Christian movies / programming.

- Stand against programming that defiles minds – write to those producers to be a voice for good.

- Join with others for creating wholesome comedy, books and film.

- Join a Christian artist association.

Pray with me: Father, release Your glory in the arts and entertainment mountain! Thank You that You delight in seeing us experience joy and happiness. Help me to break free of any shackles that have bound me in dark places with what I watch and listen too, or eat and drink. Let me run with You in every way, and in the joy set before me in Christ. In Jesus' name. Amen.

To Ponder:

- *Are you called to make a difference on this mountain of influence?*

12

SPEAK TO THE MOUNTAIN

"What are you, you great mountain? Before Zerubbabel you will become a plain; and he will bring out the top stone [finishing stone] with shouts of 'Grace, grace to it!'" – Zechariah 4:7

As we have seen, every mountain of influence has their challenges and enemies. Those enemies stand like giants bellowing their curses, demanding our servitude. But Jesus, the Son of David, has already defeated every giant seeking to rob Him of His inheritance.

As we conclude this brief look at the mountains of culture, there is one more mountain I want to look at and our needed response to it. In scripture, enemy opposition itself can be referred to as a "mountain."

In the book of Zechariah, we read about Zerubbabel, Judea's governor, and **his work to restore worship** in rebuilding Jerusalem's second Temple. Facing an onslaught of strong opposition, the full restoration began, but was delayed for eighteen years.

In the midst of overwhelming impossibilities blocking the accomplishing of his God-given task, the Lord encouraged Zerubbabel saying that the building of the temple would be finished. Worship would be restored. God's Spirit would bring the victory.

	Zerubbabel's testimony would not be his

DECLARE GOD'S GRACE OVER EVERY MOUNTAIN!

Zerubbabel's testimony would not be his own strength, but the power of *God's grace*.

"...This is the word of the Lord to Zerubbabel, 'Not by might, nor power, but by My Spirit,' says the Lord of armies." (Zech. 4:6)

Grace is the divine power for change, victory, and for establishing divine purpose. No matter the challenges in our lives, or in today's culture, there is victory!

The word **grace** (Heb. *chen*) means: *to incline towards with favor or benefit, so as to make camp with someone found acceptable and favored.* **It conveys the idea of a door of new beginnings, and chamber of life**.

In this case, God was saying, *"Zerubbabel, you have My favor! I will work on your behalf. I have made My camp with you and My presence will bring the needed victory for the work I've given you to do! Your part is to speak My power and favor over your situation."*

In other words, Zerubbabel YOU declare, *"God is with me! I have His acceptance! His purposes in this situation will succeed! His worship here will be restored! New life will come forth by the power of God's Spirit and grace ... mountains of opposition will fall!"*

This is a word to all of us, too. While we put our hands to the plow of divine labor, it is His Spirit who will bring victory as we labor to restore His worship in the earth and on every mountain of culture. Our part is to declare a door of new beginnings and the favor of God for victory. As we decree His grace to accomplish His will, *Giants will fall!*

Restoring worship on every mountain and at every gate is key to our nation's restoration. It's time to restore the altar of faith in God in our nation. So, let's declare grace over government! Grace over commerce! Grace over education! Grace over families! Grace over media! Grace over the arts and entertainment industries!

We've heard enough bad news, it's time to release the good news of glory in our midst. As we labor, we must work leaning on Jesus in everything, having His word of grace in our mouths. We must declare His goodness over every seed of divine design for every mountain. We must call it good, for God's original designs are good.

We must declare what is not yet seen, calling by faith His victory.

God has given each of us a work to do. There is a new wind of God's grace blowing on His people and the mantles He has given us for greater works. He wants His glory known! There are difficulties we will encounter, but God says to speak grace to every impossibility. Remember, this work is part of our love and worship of Him.

It doesn't matter how large or small our influence seems to us – each of us matters in our Father's Kingdom. Our work is significant for healing the world around us.

The biggest wheels of a clock won't function without the smallest wheel; we aren't responsible for the size of our influence, just our obedience.

WHERE IS YOUR FAITH FLOWING?

What do you have faith for? Where does your heart beat the most regarding the issues surrounding the seven mountains of culture? Do you feel drawn to be involved in government? In education? In business? To help families? To some area of media? Or maybe to the arts and entertainment world?

Society needs the Father's arrows to bring His glory and divine solutions to every mountain of culture.

Our salvation in Jesus Christ is more than for personal benefit. It is a life of access to divine power with a purpose that goes beyond ourselves. Our calling in Christ is bigger than us! As we grow in relationship with the Father, Son, and Holy Spirit, we will feel His heart for this world. He will help us to grow in faith and understanding that our mantles and gifts carry Kingdom significance.

We have been given spiritual authority for our lives and families and to liberate cities, regions, and nations from demonic strongholds. Every sphere of culture needs godly hearts and hands to tend them rightly that the nation might yield the fruit that glorifies our Father.

Pray with me: Father, You have made me to be a king and priest in the earth. Thank You for grace to move with Your heart and for taking Your name into the spheres of culture where You place me. May every mountain bring good news of peace to the people, and the announcement of justice. May every mountain rise to defend the oppressed among the people, to deliver the children of the poor and to crush every oppressor. Show me my part in all of this (Ps. 72:1-4). In Jesus' name. Amen (so be it)!

To Ponder:

- *What is the mountain you are called to support with divine purpose?*
- *What is the gate where Father wants you to stand and worship?*

13

GIFTED FOR A PURPOSE

"We have different gifts, according to the grace given us."
Romans 12:6a

There is a harvest not only for the souls of mankind, but for the seed of God's gifts within you. God has given you gifts, talents, and abilities that He wants you to grow in for accomplishing Kingdom purposes. These gifts will give a unique expression to the purpose of God through you.

The place where your gifts grow best is the place God has appointed for you. It is also the place where your *measure of faith* operates. Some people's faith and gifts flow strongest in the business realm. With others it's in the government realm.

For me, my gifts operate on the Faith Mountain, helping the Body of Christ grow in Him and succeed in their identity and purpose in Him. It is both my appointed place *and* how God "wired" me. My gifts are part of the heavenly blueprint He put into my personal *identity DNA*.

This identity DNA causes me to think of everything in terms of God's glory and our calling in Him. I think about people knowing God intimately and being rooted deeply in His love. It gives me vision for seeing people set free from bondage and soul wounds. I see them getting up and running in the destiny God has for them – discovering His glory in their gifts and calling. I see them making a difference! I see the glory of God on them and being released through them wherever they go.

And as I think about all this, I get excited!

God has put a heavenly blueprint into *your* personal identity DNA, too, for the work He has called you to do.

Your DNA includes your talents, abilities, and gifts for an appointed work in an appointed place. Your DNA will help give you vision for something He wants to do through your life. It will help you see a particular area that God wants to fill with His glory through your touch. It will draw your heart. That way, as you move with faith regarding it, it will be a delight to you.

You will get excited thinking about it!

YOU THINK IN THE WAY YOU WERE CREATED

Author Lance Wallnau once said, *"You think in the way that you were created for!"*

What do *you* think about?

What do you see for your life?

What do you dream about?

Whatever Kingdom work God has called you to do, you have a mantle and gifts for it.

THE TOOLS OF YOUR TRADE

Your talents and gifts are "tools" for accomplishing Kingdom purpose and assignments from the Father. Your gifts are a grace for manifesting God's glory in the earth. They are part of displaying His *manifold wisdom* before principalities and powers.

Every Kingdom endeavor needs many gifts to accomplish what God desires. Every gift, every hand, every person matters for filling the earth with God's glory,

What are your "tools"?

Some people struggle regarding their gifts and abilities. They feel like:

1. "I have no gifts."

2. "I have too many gifts; I don't know which one to grow in."

3. "I don't know where my gifts fit."

4. "I don't know how to develop my gifts."

Others are "gift saboteurs" – they sabotage their own growth and destiny because of personal strongholds.

Here are some solutions to consider for helping identify your gifts and abilities:

1. Make a list of abilities, talents, and passions.

2. Identify what God is saying to you about them and also His current assignment for you. Which gift is He highlighting as being most needed for this current assignment? I have found different gifts needed more in different seasons, depending on the assignment and what the assignment needs.

3. Identify your God-given connections and alignments. These are often key to the functioning of your gifts. Alignments with others often work to activate your gifts by putting a demand on the anointing within you. It's like they pull destiny out of you!

4. Get needed training for developing your gifts. Gifts are a responsibility and given for our work, not for hiding in a box on a shelf.

5. Break all self-limiting / self-sabotaging mindsets about yourself. Ask the Holy Spirit where strongholds may be operating, even against your ability to see or recognize your gifts. You may need some personal ministry or Christian counseling to help identify root issues and break free of strongholds.

YOU ARE UNIQUE!

Our God-given qualities set us apart from the rest of creation. They make each of us unique as God's children. As His image-bearers, we each carry the same, as well as different, characteristics. I am not you and you are not me, but we both came from God. We are both His image. We both carry His authority to rule. Even so, you have certain strengths in personality and abilities that I don't have, and vice versa.

God has unlimited gifts and no one has been left out of His gift-giving! Your gifts and abilities are both natural and spiritual that need to be developed for your unique work.

The apostle Paul said we are not to be ignorant of our gifts, and not only that, but to stir up the gift within you! (1 Cor. 12:1; 2 Tim. 1:6) Ask God what He is doing in the earth and what your part is in it. Ask Holy Spirit for wisdom regarding timing and specific action steps.

What is the cultural environment of your city or region? What needs changing that your voice, gifts, and actions will help make the difference?

Father wants to bring you into what He is doing, and Jesus wants you working side by side with Him.

Remember, you and I are the Father's resources on earth for effecting His plans. We are Jesus' hands, feet, and voice. His influence through you carries an impact on people and on culture.

You are more important than you know!

DRAWING OUT YOUR PURPOSE

Proverbs 20:5 says, "The purposes of a man's heart are deep waters, but a man of understanding draws them out." (NKJV)

While it is God who sows the seeds of destiny, gifts, and calling in our lives, we have an important part to help those seeds grow. Isaiah 61:11 says that just as the earth causes the seed inside it to sprout, and the garden causes what is sown in it to spring up, so the Lord will cause righteousness and praise to spring up in all nations.

> YOU AND I ARE TO NURTURE WHAT GOD HAS PUT IN US.

You and I are to nurture what God has put in us so that His righteousness and praise fills the earth. Father wants us to recognize the gift and purpose of God in our lives and pull it out! Push it out! Water it so that it emerges with great fruitfulness!

It is a deliberate action to pull, push, and water! It is a deliberate choice to step into our gifts and put on the mantle of anointing and authority given us.

Remember, faith has actions!

THE ANOINTING WITHIN YOUR GIFTS

There is glory in your God-given abilities because they came from Him! There is also an anointing in your gifts when you are filled with the Holy Spirit, and that anointing has a purpose. Scripture says the anointing breaks yokes of bondage. The anointing brings healing and freedom.

What freedom does God want to bring through your words and gifts? Every realm of society needs God's freedom in some way, from free speech, to right-to-life, to financial freedom, and to medical freedom, to name a few.

> THERE IS AN ANOINTING IN YOUR GIFTS ... AND THAT ANOINTING HAS A PURPOSE!

Lord, help us see what we have not yet seen, and our part in being Your healing and freedom agents.

In this hour, Jesus is putting a fresh demand on the anointing He's given us. It's time, He says, for My body to step into full function!

I learned the importance of stepping into full function through an experience I had some years ago. I was invited to participate on a ministry team that operated with an anointing I felt was stronger than what I carried. I felt like a minnow among whales. We were in a time of ministry and they had called a woman to the front to pray for her. My thought was just to add my faith through simply being present ... until they handed me the mic to prophetically pray over her. Without even thinking I shook my head that I had nothing to pray and so passed the mic to someone else.

In that moment the Lord spoke loud and clear to me, "Did you even ask ME if I had something to say to her?" I was immediately convicted. I had not even asked the Lord regarding this individual and what He might want to say. I had NO

174

expectation of any demand on the anointing given me for the position God gave me.

I repented and asked the Lord what He wanted to say for the woman. He gave me a word and when the mic was available, I grabbed it and prayed! I stepped into my identity and God's purpose for me on that team. As soon as I released what God gave me, boom! The power of God hit that woman in a way she had not experienced before ... per her words.

All God wants is our willingness and faith, not in ourselves, but in Him. If we ask, He will supply what is needed for what He wants to do through you and me.

It's not about us, but simply showing up, owning the gift and position we are given, and letting the Holy Spirit move through us. We must look to Him with expectation that He will! We are to stir up the gift within us for the purpose it was given!

I love what Life Coach Valerie Burton says:

**"Your gifts and talents are a gift from God –
what you do with them is your gift to Him."**

YOUR GIFT MAKES ROOM FOR YOU

Proverbs 18:16 says, *"A man's gift makes room for him, and brings him before great men."* When your gifts and abilities are developed, they will place you in unique places and positions for a divine purpose. They will place you in your appointed place, just like God appointed a place for Adam.

Your gifts will carry you into specific realms of relationship and influence for effecting God's purposes. They will release redemptive purposes into situations to bring freedom and healing to people. They will destroy wicked works and build God's designs.

YOUR GIFTS WILL CARRY YOU INTO SPECIFIC REALMS OF RELATION-SHIP AND INFLUENCE FOR EFFECTING GOD'S PURPOSES.

That is why it's important to develop your gifts. To own them. To stir them to action with faith!

Again, gifts and abilities (natural and spiritual) are like seeds that need to be developed. They are nurtured through development and **practice** to help draw out the purpose of God for them and in them. That purpose will manifest more as we embrace God-given alignments, God's timing, and God's location for us.

Gifts are also part of your mantle.

IDENTIFYING YOUR GIFTS

1. Talent, Natural Gifts, and Abilities

To gain clarity about your gifts, it can be helpful to make a list of all the gifts you know of, or anything you have been good at. Everyone has a natural talent or ability. It is sometimes not recognized but it is there. Talents can be identified as something that comes natural to you. It might be that you are good with words, organization, math, music, languages, strategies, event planning, or historical research, etc. Or, you might be good at drawing or painting, technology, leadership, working with specific age groups like children, youth, or older people.

Gifts include a vast number of things. Ask yourself, what activity feels like your *sweet spot*? Even natural gifts are given for a purpose to manifest the works of God in the earth.

Make a list.

Things I am good at:_____

_____

_____

_____

_____

_____

_____

_____

Also, how do your talents link to a mountain of influence? Are you good at languages but want to help bring positive change to government? Maybe you could be a government translator. Are you a story writer who likes to inspire young people with courage, hope, or vision for their life? Or maybe you like doing videos and would be good at helping create inspiring programs.

If you aren't sure what your natural talents are, ask the Holy Spirit to show you. Here are some questions to also help:

1. What do you like to do?

2. What do others say you are good at?

3. What have you done that felt fulfilling and delightful when doing it?

4. What words have been spoken over your life that you knew were from God regarding gifts or purpose?

5. What ability do you feel God prompting you to use to help bring change somewhere?

As you clarify your answers on these, write a personal purpose statement. For example: God wants me to use my gift of _____ to help / serve _____ to accomplish _____. (_An example might be: God wants me to use my gift of marketing to help a Christian non-profit organization accomplish their mission to bring people out of poverty_).

2. Gifts of Breakthrough

List places where you have gained victory or breakthrough in your life. Every struggle you've walked through and gained victory in is an area where you have also gained spiritual authority and knowledge. God often uses us in these areas to bring breakthrough for others:

_____

_____

_____

_____

_____

_____

_____

3. Dreams and Desires

List desires and dreams that keep popping up in your thoughts over and over.

_____

_____

_____

_____

_____

_____

_____

4. Prophetic Words

List any words that God has spoken to you, whether directly to your heart or through His Word, or through someone else where your spirit felt a witness that the word was from God. Prophetic words should always bring comfort, confirmation, and exhortation; never condemnation or confusion. What has God spoken to you?

Make a list.

_____

_____

_____

_____

_____

_____

_____

5. Redemptive Gifts

In the New Testament there are three lists of spiritual gifts. The first list is in Romans 12:3-8. It is a list of gifts from the Father. Many call these *redemptive gifts* and reflect the Father's own nature. These gifts are: *prophet, server, teacher, exhorter, ruler (leader), giver, and mercy.* A redemptive gift is reflected in how you are "wired" from birth. It is part of your inherent nature.

A redemptive gift filters the way you see and interpret life and circumstances. It motivates how you respond to situations, and what is meaningful to you. It creates a framework through which you engage and use your other gifts, talents, and abilities, and how you *perceive and respond to the Father's purposes* in the earth. Typically, a person is strongest in one or two of the redemptive gifts.

Here is a brief description of how the redemptive gifts function:

- **The prophet gift** – someone with this gift sees the big picture of God's designs and purposes. Their revelatory insight motivates a passion to see those designs come into fullness, and be free from any hindrance. They are *design* and *purpose* oriented.

(Note: the *redemptive gift of prophet* is not the same as the *equipping gift of prophet* listed in Ephesians 4:11. Jesus' *equipping gift of prophet* is someone who delivers a word from God for a person, place, or regarding a future event.)

- **The servant gift** – someone with this gift perceives the need for practical helps. They see what services are needed and are concerned with details for plans and purposes to succeed. They are helps and service oriented.

- **The teacher gift** – someone with this gift perceives the need for people to know and understand their individual responsibility regarding God's designs and plans, helping them to know their part and how to function in them. They are skill and instruction oriented.

- **The exhorter gift** – someone with this gift perceives people's need for encouragement, for emotional and spiritual support, and for endurance in life and God's plans for them. They are faith and courage oriented.

- **The giver gift** – someone with this gift perceives the need of resources for God's plans and designs to succeed. They have a passion to give finances, and provide supplies where needed, and for Kingdom advancement. They are giving oriented.

- **The ruler gift** – someone with this gift perceives the need for leadership and right order for successful function of God's designs and plans. They are leadership and order oriented.

- **The mercy gift** – someone with this gift perceives the need for the fulfillment of the heart's desires. They are compassionate and motivated to see the heart's desire fulfilled, beginning with God's heart. They are heart and relationship oriented.

Looking at the redemptive gifts, it's easy to see all of them in operation in the life of Jesus: as **Prophet**, He ministered the designs of God and called people into their destiny; He came as a **Servant**, **Teaching** the people and **Exhorting** them with great words of encouragement.

Jesus was the greatest **Giver** of all, even giving of His own life for our full restoration. As **Ruler**, He brought order to the chaos of people's minds and hearts as He ministered the everlasting **Mercies** of God, putting His own blood on the mercy seat that we might experience fulfillment through intimate fellowship with God.

Every area of culture needs the operation of *all* the redemptive gifts to release the blessing of God – that is their purpose.

The following is an example of how these gifts might work in a practical way. Imagine someone who feels led by God to launch a Christian television station as a means to bring God's blessing to the region. This person would need people with other gifts to help advance this vision and its intended blessing. This is how the 7 redemptive gifts might function together:

- The prophet gift sees God's design for the station and its impact in the region, the type of programming needed, etc. that will release God's heart and blessing. That gift provides an understanding of what God wants and a blueprint for success.

- The servant brings in practical helps, such as a secretary, camera man, set designer, cleaning crew, etc.

- The giver helps finance the blessing of God through buildings, equipment, microphones, cameras, etc.

- The ruler advances the blessing through leadership in effectively running operations.

- The teacher trains and equips individuals for their skilled positions needed to advance God's purposes, perhaps consulting, coaching, or writing operation manuals.

- The exhorter might be the TV show host who shares the station's message.

- The mercy gift prays and intercedes for the station to succeed, or they may be the creative marketer, the fashion artist who helps TV hosts dress their best, set décor, etc., to make sure the purpose is fulfilled.

Imagine with me another example:

A group of men and women representing all seven gifts walk into a restaurant. They are hungry and ready to eat but find chaos, poor service, poor food, and frazzled and overworked waiters. Here's how the seven might respond:

After sitting in the restaurant for 20 minutes with no water, menu, or waiter, the prophet watches and notices the poor layout of the premise. He is already thinking of a better layout to prevent possible accidents to the waiters. Suddenly, not to his surprise, two waiters collide with trays in hand. The prophet seeks out the manager to recommend a better design for his restaurant, while the servant helps the waiters clean up the mess.

The teacher gives instruction to the waiters about social awareness, while the ruler tells everyone to stay calm, stay seated, and then asks who is in charge so he can give them tips on better leadership. The exhorter encourages the waiter that everything is going to be okay, while the mercy gift prays for everyone's peace. After lunch, the giver pays the tab for everyone and gives a generous tip to the waiter, regardless of the chaos and poor food, knowing it would bless the waiter who was having a bad day.

Which action best describes you? Seeing potential problems? Helping with the mess? Taking charge? Encouraging the waiter? Praying for everyone's peace? Paying and giving a generous tip?

What is your redemptive gift?

If you are unsure, good resources include Arthur Burk's materials at Sapphire Leadership Group (https://theslg.com), and Johnny Enlow's ministry at Rise Global Community (www.rise7.org). Rise7 also has an app with a free assessment to help you determine your redemptive gift and the mountain you are called to impact.

A **free redemptive assessment** can also be taken online at: www.high5test.com.

List your two main redemptive gifts:

_____

_____

6. Spiritual Gifts

The second set of biblical gifts are ones that the Holy Spirit gives us (see 1 Corinthians 12:4-11). These are *spiritual gifts* given to every believer to *manifest the works of the Holy Spirit* in the earth. These include:

- Words of wisdom
- Words of knowledge
- Faith
- Healings
- Miracles
- Prophecy
- Discernment of spirits

- Tongues
- Interpretation of tongues

As mentioned, spiritual gifts are given to us by the Holy Spirit to empower our ministry calling and purpose for advancing the Father's Kingdom. Each gift is equally valuable. Exercising our gifts help us develop in spiritual maturity.

To know your gift, take a spiritual gifts assessment and list your 3 *highest* gifts: (go to: https://giftstest.com/allgifts)

My spiritual gifts are:

_____

_____

_____

_____

_____

7. Equipping Gifts

The third set of biblical gifts is found in Ephesians 4:7-8. These are called *spiritual equipping gifts* from Jesus for the training of His Ekklesia. Earlier we mentioned these gifts as those who train and grow the Body of Christ.

These gifts are given to develop and mature the saints so that every member of His Body is growing to full maturity of faith, *and* in the ministry God has for them.

These are:

- **Apostles** – ones sent to establish God's Kingdom government, authority, and culture in regions.
- **Prophets** – ones appointed to declare God's will, and release His power.

- **Evangelists** – ones who share the good news of Christ and call people into God's Kingdom.

- **Pastors** – ones appointed to feed God's people with His Word and care for their spiritual growth.

- **Teachers** – ones appointed to train God's people in His ways.

Again, these gifts don't just do the work of ministry, but they equip God's people to do the work of ministry as an apostolic, prophetic, evangelistic, shepherding, and discipling family going into every sphere of culture to bring divine transformation.

Apostles *equip* people to help to establish God's Kingdom in their regions. Prophets *equip* people to hear God and move on what He says. Evangelists *equip* believers to share the gospel. Pastors don't just lead and nurture God's people, but *equip* them to nurture others in God's love and truth. Teachers *equip and train* God's people to walk in His ways for a life of faith and greater works.

Has Jesus called you as one of these *spiritual equippers?*

8. Personality and Motivational Gifts

There are many other ways to assess what you are best suited for. Just by identifying how you are wired helps you develop what is already inside you.

Other online assessments that can benefit your journey of discovery include:

- Jung Personality Test (123test.com)
- CliftonStrengths (see store.gallup.com)
- DISC profile assessment

You can look all of these up on the internet. These assessments will give you both insight and confirmation of how God designed you.

I have worked with many people seeking direction who find these tools very helpful. Some have gone on to begin their own businesses as they discover who they are. As with all things, these are just part our Kingdom identity and purpose.

DEVELOPING IN YOUR GIFTS

With all gifts comes responsibility as in the parable of the ten talents. The bottom line is, who does Father want you to help? What mountain does He want to touch through you to help bring change?

Developed gifts open the door for you to fill the place you are intended to occupy. There are many ways and resources to hone your abilities, once you recognize what they are. This is especially important for parents and leaders wanting to develop the lives under their care.

Abba Father wants us to be sharp arrows that hit the target of divine purpose.

Here are some tips for developing your gifts:

1. *Pray and search* for right resources and training.
2. *Get specialized* training to unlock your potential.
3. *Keep up-to-date* with new skills and technology.
4. *Understand* the law of sacrifice – there is a cost to the mastery of skills, including time, finances, and practical application.
5. *Decide* to be a person of influence to make a difference.
6. *Write the vision, make it plain, so you can run your course.* (Habakkuk 2:2)

- What is your vision?

- What change do you want to see happen and how can your voice and gifts help?

- How has your history and journey in life developed you for your place or role now?

- Where are you called to build? Change? Influence? Support? Help transform?

- What needs to be further developed in your life?

- What alignments need strengthened or let go?

- Write a vision / mission statement about what you see and what is your part in seeing it come to pass.

Your gifts are like wheels that give you movement for your Kingdom purpose. They place you on the mountain (or sphere) appointed for you. They are the means by which you fly as the Father's arrow.

If you are a parent, pay attention to the gifts that are trying to find expression through your child's interests and abilities. Help them increase in that area.

> YOUR GIFTS ARE LIKE WHEELS THAT GIVE YOU MOVEMENT FOR YOUR KINGDOM PURPOSES.

Whatever gift you have, use it for God's glory. If it is writing then write, inventing then invent, organizing then organize, singing then sing, doctoring, then be a doctor God's way, or lawyering then do it to further true justice.

Whatever you do, do it with all your strength, *and* with the anointing of the Holy Spirit!

No matter what or how many gifts we have, they cannot fully accomplish heaven's designs for earth without the anointing of the Holy Spirit. Let Him guide, direct and empower every gift you have been given as you humbly submit to Him.

THE GIFT OF PRAISE

There is one final gift that everyone has been given, and that is the ability to give God praise in all things. It is the gift we give to Him in exalting Him above everything else.

Scripture says to sing unto the Lord, sing praises to His name – to exalt Him and rejoice before Him. If we want His presence in our life and sphere of influence, then praise Him, for He inhabits our praise! (Ps. 22:3)

Every one of us has a voice to speak and to sing. Some have beautiful voices. Some can't carry a tune. Regardless, we delight the heart of God when we sing His praises in every situation, and on every mountain.

When we declare God's worth through our praise, it shifts atmospheres in our soul, in our homes, and even in our regions. It releases the power of His presence. It fills the earth with His glory.

Over the past few years, worship leader, Sean Feucht, has travelled America releasing worship through large open-air events to shift the spiritual atmosphere over cities. Others I know have also travelled across the nation releasing the song of the Lord over the land and rivers – their worship and intercession releasing the purifying sound of heaven over cities and regions.

We, too, can shift atmospheres over regions through our prayers, actions, declarations and praise. Imagine singing God's praises to invite His glory into your classroom, boardroom, senate chamber, or place of work!

We can shift atmospheres as we praise Him in our homes, in our cars, and throughout our day! Our song may be loud or soft, but just think what it would look like if we all released the song of the Lord wherever we went ... the earth would be filled with His glory, just like heaven.

Pray with me: *Father, thank You for all the gifts You have given me. Help me to see their value, my value, and my part in filling the earth with Your glory. Teach me to release Your praise wherever I go. In Jesus' name. Amen.*

To Ponder:

- *What are your gifts?*
- *Have you decided to release His praise wherever you go?*

14

MOBILIZING TO MAKE A DIFFERENCE

"May the God who gives endurance and encouragement give you a spirit of unity among yourselves as you follow Christ Jesus, so that with one heart and mouth you may glorify the God and Father of our Lord Jesus Christ." – Romans 15:5-6

Whatever God calls you to do, it will be connected to a community. God is a God of community. He works in community. He builds through community. Jesus ministered to His region through the community of His disciples. When He sent them out, they went two by two. No one was alone.

Paul exhorts us to not forsake the fellowship with believers because we have something to both give *and* to receive in community. We are to accept one another as Christ accepted us.

As the Body of Christ, we are many members. A Body functions together for a purpose. We can never attain to the fullness of God's purposes apart from connection with others. No one develops or matures independent of community. Cultural reformation cannot happen by one person alone. It needs the unity and mobilization of all believers.

THE IMPORTANCE OF ALIGNMENT

The advancement of the Father's Kingdom will be through a company of people, a family and army of sons and daughters who are deeply rooted in the Father's love and who love one another. God wants His family to move together *as one*.

This includes the unity and movement of the generations together, seeking God's heart to fill the earth with His glory. Each one bringing their gifts as a supply to the whole Body.

GOD IS RAISING A COMPANY OF LEADERS WHO WILL MOVE WITH COURAGE.

Through the years, God has given me a number of prophetic dreams and visions regarding His heart for unity. I wrote about one of them in my book, *Breaking the Silence,* where God showed me that He is bringing forth a "*Gad*" generation.

Gad was one of the tribes of Israel described as warriors and leaders, and whose faces were like lions. The symbol of that tribe was a camp with many tents.

God is raising a company of leaders who will move with courage, love, and boldness to overcome evil. They will rise as a new Godly leadership in the earth.

In another dream, God showed me that He is forming a "*Joshua company.*" It is a company that will move with the heart and presence of the Father, Son, and Holy Spirit, and will increase (multiply) in every way, and not decrease. They will move to establish God's glory in the land.

In the Old Testament, Joshua didn't go in alone to bring cultural change to Canaan. He went in with an army of God's people, each one doing their part to remove evil from the land, taking the ark of God's glory with them.

Another time, I had a vision of Jesus sitting on the beach mending a net. I asked Him what He was doing. He smiled and replied, "A net-work!" Today, Jesus is doing a great network with His people. Because of the great needs our nation is facing, we must come together. We must break past doctrinal differences and join hands for the common purposes of Christ for our cities, regions, and nation.

We are in an hour where *together we make a difference*. We can no longer afford to carry grudges, offenses, jealousies, or unholy divisions. We can no longer walk in rejection or isolation.

We must break free of pride and selfish ambition, seeking the honor of Jesus alone ... and not our own.

Selfish ambition and building personal fame is a *religious spirit* that has brought much destruction and heartache to the Body of Christ. We must grow up and honor one another for the glory of *His* name, not ours.

This is the hour to walk in love and grace as we seek the manifestation of *His* Kingdom and righteousness – preferring one another as we bring our gifts, and receive the gift of God in others, too.

> TOGETHER
> WE MAKE
> A
> DIFFERENCE!

On the night of the Last Supper, Jesus talked heart-to-heart with His disciples. He told them to love one another. He prayed the Father would make them one in Him, just as He (Jesus) and the Father are one. The early Church was marked by a great love for one another. They had one focus – to see the King and His Kingdom manifest on earth.

There is coming a fresh movement of love and unity to Christ's Body for end-time ministry. For that to happen, He is sending His fire to cleanse the motives of our hearts from all self-seeking. He knows that where there is selfish ambition there is confusion and every evil thing (James 3:16). We cannot have every evil thing *and* God's glory.

Philippians 2:3 says, *"Do nothing from selfishness or empty conceit, but with humility consider one another as more important than yourselves."* We must ask Holy Spirit to help us discern the motives of our own hearts.

> WE WERE CREATED TO BELONG.

As Jesus unifies and networks His Body, He will connect each of us with specific relationships. Knowing your calling and gifts will help you recognize your role in that relationship, and the purpose for the favor you are given.

Be aware of the favor for the position God gives you for Kingdom assignments. Recognize, too, that the enemy will try to get you out of right alignment. Look for relationships with pure hearted people pursuing the heart of God as you follow the Holy Spirit's leading.

It is a time to be focused and rightly aligned for your assignment. Assignments can change in different seasons, so realize that relationships and alignments can also change according to the season. Watch for God's confirmation, and never be moved by offense.

UNIFIED FOR A PURPOSE

Any large and difficult task is made easier by more hands. No one person can solve today's social issues. Like ancient Israel, our warfare for the land will not be won without God's manifest glory, and each one doing our part with Him.

194

For the past number of years people have been abandoning churches, for many reasons. One being they are tired of seeker friendly ministries that have no vision for either true personal change or for cultural transformation. Others have left not knowing where they fit. Destiny and purpose is beating in them to know *Who am I? What am I to do? And where is my tribe – my community where I fit? Where do I make a difference?*

Do you know where you fit? Here are some thoughts to consider:

- Take a moment to identify the relationships and community where you are. Is it a God-given alignment, or are you just filling a need to belong?
- What is your relationship to that community?
- Are you stepping fully into the gift that you bring to that community for advancing God's purposes?
- Is there a gift in you that needs activating for your part in that community?

If you don't know some of the answers to these questions, ask Holy Spirit about the alignments and community He has for you, and your role in them.

Communities can include a local Church body, a home fellowship, a Christian organization with a Kingdom goal, or a special ministry where you are connected.

A BODY HAS MANY MEMBERS

We were created to belong, and every one of our gifts are important to the Body as a whole. 1 Corinthians 12 says that the Body is not one member, but many. Each part (member) has a supply to bring to the rest.

That supply comes through the anointing and gifts flowing through each one. The other "body parts" help to draw out the

195

anointing within us, just as natural body parts give and receive from each other, causing the whole body to move and be full of life. This is why identifying your gifts and developing them is so important. We were each created to be a supply to others and to receive the supply of God through them.

Kingdom purposes often go undone because someone doesn't show up. The Church is to be Jesus' supply of good to the nations, but that is hindered when body parts are missing!

Today, there is a great activation of Christ's Body and the anointed mantles we carry. "Body parts" are getting into place for full function as God's glory is being outpoured!

OVERCOMING DISCONNECTION

There are many reasons that keep people from connecting fully with God and others. If this is you, ask Holy Spirit if any of the following is something that applies to you. If not, be aware of helping others break free of any of these hindrances:

1. You don't believe in who you are.

2. You don't have a hopeful perspective, so what does it matter?

3. You don't know what to do.

4. You're just trying to survive where you are.

5. You hold back because there are so many others doing something similar to what's in your heart, making you feel like your part is insignificant.

6. You've been taught doctrines that don't value the Church's part in culture beyond their own personal salvation.

7. You're just waiting for the rapture because the anti-Christ is going to destroy everything anyway... hopefully you'll make it out in time.

Father wants you to believe in Him AND in who He uniquely designed you to be as His son or daughter. No one can supply exactly what you bring to this world in the way you bring it. No one.

Redemption isn't just about our rescue, but the restoration of the whole earth and everything in it. And, by the way, the book of Revelation isn't about the anti-Christ, it is the revelation of JESUS CHRIST! Let's not magnify the wicked one.

With Jesus there is always a hopeful future. He has already defeated Satan. He is the Triumphant One. There is power in His name. There is power in His blood. There is power to overcome evil. There is a whole heavenly host more in number with Jesus and with us, than those against us.

We need to remember that. And too, we have one another!

The Holy Spirit is moving. It's time to stir up the gift within you. Believe in your calling. Have faith in God, not in the devil. Do God's will for your life, your home, your city, region, and nation. Their well-being needs you!

STRATEGIZE AND MOBILIZE

Here are some more things to consider regarding what God is saying and how He wants to mobilize us in this hour:

1. Know the "seasonal" expression of your purpose to your generation. What is God doing now?

2. In what ways are you connecting with others on the mountain where you want to see change?

3. Where do you need to change your perspective for expanding your possibilities?

4. Ask Holy Spirit to help you think more creatively! Challenge old paradigms.

5. Clarify obstacles.

6. Realize that momentum is created by incremental changes; momentum is also created by intentional focus and action. Success is not an accident.

7. Desire to *and* decide to be a *change agent*. Hunger for a changed world!

8. Value yourself and value people – they are God's creation, as are you.

9. Get over yourself; when you fall, get up! The world needs you.

10. Pray for your sphere of influence.

11. Seek revelation for your assignment; pray for divine strategies and blueprints.

12. Write a personal mission statement, one that carries a plan of action.

ANSWERING THE CALL

Father sent you here, at this time, to make a difference!

Commit to fully being who God created you to be. Commit to your own growth and transformation in His glory. A transformed individual creates a transformed world.

There is an anointing and divine power designed to move through your life for manifesting the Father's Kingdom on earth as it is in heaven. Your gifts, voice, and connections are the tools for taking down demonic strongholds and for building Father's designs on earth. This is who we are as His sons and daughters!

God is raising His family to fill the earth with His glory. Just look at what we have been given for this purpose:

- Living waters to share! (John 4:14)
- Power and authority as the sons and daughters of God! (John 1:12)
- Keys of the Kingdom! (Matt. 16:19)
- A divine commission to disciple nations! (Matt. 28:19)
- An anointing to heal and set captives free! (Matt. 10:8)
- The Holy Spirit who gives us power for our Kingdom labor! (John 14:16-17; Acts 1:8)
- Irresistible wisdom! (Luke 21:15)
- Whatever we ask in His name! (John 16:23)

How can we lose? How much more do we need? These alone are more than enough to *"turn the world upside down!"*

THE RISE OF REVIVALISTS AND REFORMERS

God is raising up an army of revivalists and reformers. Your role and voice matter. Perhaps *you* will be the next Billy Graham or Oral Roberts. Or perhaps the next Harriet Tubman who freed people trapped in slavery. Maybe you will bring justice for the children like Edgar G. Murphy, a minister in Alabama who advocated legislation to stop child labor abuse.

Perhaps you will be another Janet Porter who wrote the "Heartbeat Bill" and helped put a stop to abortion. Or maybe you'll be like Charlie Kirk and help train young people as freedom activists.

Reformers come from all walks of life and move in myriad ways for righteousness. Some are frontline faces, while others are behind the scenes. Some are well-known, most aren't. The earth is reeling from evil agendas but victories *will* happen (and many are) as Christ's Body puts on their mantles and seeks His Kingdom first.

Today, stopping tyranny inspired by forces from hell is not an option. The harvest is ready and people are desperate for hope in the midst of a global oppression impacting health, business, family and finances on every level. It's time for us to stand at the gates and let the God of glory into our spheres.

STEPPING INTO YOUR KINGDOM IDENTITY AND PURPOSE

The truth is that only Jesus can fill the earth with God's glory. He is the glory of the Father and the King of glory. While He sovereignly moves through outpourings of His Spirit to do so, He still calls us to partner with Him in this.

Remember, as Psalm 115:16 says, *"The earth He has given to the sons of men."* The question is, what will we do with it? More importantly, what will we do as the Body of the Son of Man to whom the earth belongs? Now is the time for the "Gads" to rise and the "Joshua generation" to move with courage to restore God's glory on every mountain of culture.

The gates of Hell are open and streams of wickedness are pouring like rivers over the nation. Do you know who you are yet? Do you know your purpose? Millions are waiting for help and hope – for the glory to appear as heaven's portals open through godly worship and action at the gates.

Every sphere of culture – government, family, business, education, media, arts & entertainment, and faith – are in transition. Concerted evil has been pulling them into a downward spiral to hell; **it's time to pull them up into the glory realms!** The mountains are waiting for the presence of God. They are waiting for the peace of God.

200

Amos 9 prophesies of the time when David's Tabernacle will be restored, and when nations will come into their proper alignment to bear God's name and glory. That Tabernacle speaks of the government of the Son of David restoring God's glory in our midst ... so that the Father's *glory becomes the center upon which our lives turn.* **Then the mountains will drip with new wine!**[1]

Jesus is calling us to join Him in the reality of who we are in Him. Our Christian experience is not complete if our salvation is only about us. We have not only died and risen to new life in Christ, but we have been seated with Him in heavenly places – places of authority over principalities and powers for prospering and protecting the seed of life and land.

We must stop thinking that it is up to someone else to cover the earth with God's glory ... to let someone else don the robe of *their* anointing while the mantle given us hangs in the closet.

You and I matter! Our identity and purpose matters!

The gates of heaven are open wide for full access to God's glory for walking fully in our Kingdom identity and purpose.

Will you labor with Jesus for the harvest He desires?

Will you step fully into who you are and why you are here?

If not you, who? If not now, when?

Pray with me: Father, You have brought me into this world for such a time as this. You have mantled me to bring Your light where it is dark. Teach me to pick up the Kingdom mantle You've given me and run with it! No more wondering, delaying, or living for my own benefit. I am Your shadow – teach me to move with You "as one." May You be the center upon which my life turns as I seek first Your Kingdom on earth as it is in heaven. In Jesus' name. So be it.

ENDNOTES

INTRODUCTION
[1] https://www.barna.com/research/competing-worldviews-influence-todays-christians/

https://www.arizonachristian.edu/2022/05/12/shocking-lack-of-biblical-worldview-among-american-pastors/

CHAPTER 1
[1] Fuchsia Pickett, *Placed in His Glory,* Charisma House. 2021.Pp 4.
[2] https://www.foxnews.com/media/florida-father-daughter-suicide-school-counseling-gender-identity
[3] https://www.nbcnews.com/feature/nbc-out/comedian-s-death-underscores-high-suicide-rate-among-transgender-people-n1067546
[4] https://www.pinknews.co.uk/2021/08/24/trans-suicide-four-times-rate/
[5] John 3:3 (NET); Phil. 3:20 (NET); Gal. 4:26; 2 Cor. 5:20

CHAPTER 2
[1] Cindy Jacobs, *Reformers Arise.* Destiny Image, Shippensburg, PA. 2021. PP 208-209

CHAPTER 3
[1] http://www.macollege.in/app/webroot/uploads/department_materials/doc_460.pdf
[2] Ephesians 6:20
[3] Exod. 23:28-31; Num. 33:52, 55; Lev 18:24; Deut. 7:22, 16; 20:17; Deut. 33:27; Josh. 24:12; Judg. 2:3; 6:9; 11:23–24; Amos 2:9; Ps. 78:55; 80:9; 1 Chron. 17:21; 2 Chron. 20:7
[4] Judg. 1:1 – 2:5; Ps. 106:34-35

CHAPTER 4

[1] Michael S. Heiser, *Reversing Hermon: Enoch, the Watchers, and the Forgotten Mission of Jesus Christ,* Defender Publishing, 2017.

[2] https://ephraimintheland.wordpress.com/2019/01/03/the-revelation-of-the-name-yhvh/

[3] http://nebula.wsimg.com/2c2f25206362abee7844f4bb24e11bf6?AccessKeyId=D40106E1331C24ABD7C3&disposition=0&alloworigin=1

[4] Ezekiel 29:3-4, Job 34, Revelation 17:1-2, Revelation 12:12 and 1 Samuel 5:3

[5] https://www.the7mountains.com/history-of-the-7-mountains

[6] https://www.nationalreview.com/corner/maryland-bill-effectively-decriminalizes-neglecting-newborns-to-death/

CHAPTER 5

[1] https://resources.cfni.org/resources/voicemagazine/CFNI_Magazine_201303.pdf

CHAPTER 7

[1] https://time.com/5891261/early-american-education-history/

[2] https://www.nas.org/blogs/article/u_s_founding_fathers_on_education_in_their_own_words

[3] https://time.com/5891261/early-american-education-history/

[4] https://www.goodreads.com/quotes/3238296-i-am-much-afraid-that-the-universities-will-prove-to

[5] https://scripturenuggets.wordpress.com/2013/10/29/moments-of-truth-the-perizzites-2/

CHAPTER 8

[1] Beverley Watkins & Robert Henderson, *The Trading Floors of Heaven.*

[2] https://www.state.gov/humantrafficking-about-human-trafficking/

CHAPTER 9

[1] https://www.evergreenpsychotherapycenter.com/importance-touch/

[2] https://www.theatlantic.com/magazine/archive/2020/07/can-an-unloved-child-learn-to-love/612253/

[3] https://americafirstpolicy.com/latest/20220215-fatherlessness-and-its-effects-on-american-society

[4] https://www.evergreenpsychotherapycenter.com/attachment-therapy/traits-disrupted-attachment/

[5] https://www.nbcdfw.com/news/local/advocacy-group-reads-names-of-27000-dallas-county-children-abused-in-2021/2936092/

[6] https://www.theepochtimes.com/chapter-seven-destruction-of-the-family-part-i_2661675.html

[7] https://en.wikipedia.org/wiki/Šauška

[8] https://answersingenesis.org/holidays/easter/is-the-name-easter-of-pagan-origin/
   https://www.worldhistory.org/ishtar/

CHAPTER 10

[1] Matt. 14:25; Mark 4:39; Matt. 8:28-34

[2] Masaru Emoto, *The Miracle of Water*, Atria Books. 2011.

[3] Leviticus 6:2, Masoretic Text, Strong's Concordance 3584

[4] http://injesus.com/message-archives/prophetic/Frontlines/girgashite-spirit-going-back-to-the-filth-god-saved

CHAPTER 11

[1] https://www.lifesize.com/en/blog/speaking-without-words/

CHAPTER 14

[1] 1 Chron. 16; Isa. 16;5; Amos 9:11-15; Acts 15:16

ABOUT THE AUTHOR

J. Nicole Williamson, founder of King's Lantern Ministries, is an apostolic teacher, minister, Identity & Purpose Coach, and founder of *The Healing Place* (a ministry of inner healing and spiritual freedom). Her passion is to see God's glory manifest in the nations as God's people rise in their true identity, purpose, and authority in Christ. Her revelatory teachings and books help people discover the richness of their identity and purpose, experience fresh freedom and wholeness, and advance with a biblical worldview for cultural transformation.

She and her husband, Ken, are aligned with CFN-FMC, FMCI, Glory of Zion International, and KingdomLife Christian Center. They live in the Dallas, TX area.

For more information on J. Nicole Williamson go to:
www.kingslantern.com

If you would like to invite the author to speak to your group, or to hold a seminar at your location, write to:
nicole@kingslantern.com

OTHER BOOKS BY J. NICOLE WILLIAMSON

Breaking the Silence
(Taking a stand for Life, Liberty, and all Things Good)

The Believer's Identity Devotional Handbook
(120 "I am" Statements of a Christian)

Life with Abba Father
(Fathered by God for a Divine Purpose)

The Empowered Woman
(Restoring Women to Their True Identity)

Heaven's Secret of Success
(Growing in Your Identity to Full Potential)

The Esther Mandate
(The War for America's Destiny)

Freedom in the Light
(Engaging the Truth that Sets You Free:
a Jesus Centered 12-Step Program)

SEMINARS & COURSES

Empowered for Destiny Seminar
(12 hour Inner Healing & Deliverance Ministry and Training)

Mending Hearts – Freeing Captives
(15 hour online course in biblical counsel and inner healing)

Made in the USA
Columbia, SC
10 August 2022